# THE
# OVERNIGHT
# CONSULTANT

# THE OVERNIGHT CONSULTANT

Marsha D. Lewin

JOHN WILEY & SONS, INC.

New York • Chichester • Brisbane • Toronto • Singapore

Copyright © 1995 by Marsha D. Lewin.
Published by John Wiley & Sons, Inc.

*Library of Congress Cataloging-in-Publication Data:*

Lewin, Marsha D.
     The overnight consultant / Marsha Lewin.
         p.   cm.
     Includes index.
     ISBN 0-471-11944-X (cloth).—ISBN 0-471-11945-8 (paper).
     1. Business consultants—Handbooks, manuals, etc.   I. Title.
   HD69.C6L44   1996
   001—dc20                                              95-17526

Printed in the United States of America
10  9  8  7  6  5  4  3  2  1

*To David, for his love and support*

# PREFACE

So you want to become a management consultant, do you? Perhaps you've quit your job (or had your job suddenly quit on you), or you're about to do so, and the siren call of consulting beckons to you. And you want—*and need*—as much information as you can get to make sure that the move is successful, profitable, and enjoyable from the start. You don't have time to waste on mistakes; you need information immediately on how to leverage your particular skills and experience so that you can become the best consultant you can possibly be, and as quickly as possible.

Rather than learning these lessons myself through trial and error over a quarter of a century, I would have relished a practical guide to help me through the maze of business issues that consultants face. I wish when I had started that there had been a book that outlined what the profession really entailed, what business management skills are needed, what the real issues are that contribute to success, and what the future might look like within the profession.

# PREFACE

Thus was the idea of *The Overnight Consultant* born. In this book, I've distilled decades of combined experience of other notable consultants into a primer for readers who are anxious to spend their time practicing the craft of consulting rather than researching the field (and possibly losing the golden moment). As our fast-paced society now demands, today's consultant must get started quickly—and in the right direction.

I've organized *The Overnight Consultant* into three parts that facilitate locating the information you'll need to get yourself jump-started in your new career:

1. What you need to know *tonight*.
2. What you need to do *tomorrow*.
3. What you need to know *in the long term* in order to run a consulting practice successfully.

You can read the parts you most need to get you going as quickly and competently as possible and deal with the most pressing concerns and issues right away.

Part One addresses the factors that go into deciding whether becoming a consultant is a good idea—for *you*. It talks to the professional persona, the expectations, and what you need to do to get started. It takes you through conducting assignments—the first one and successive ones.

Part Two deals with the business practice issues of the consultant. Although these issues are common to most solo-based professional service organizations, their successful mastery is critical for any consultant. I treat here in greater detail the concepts I introduced in Part One.

Part Three addresses the longer-term principles that affect your choice of consulting as a lifetime's work. These principles clearly and unequivocally require mastery early in a consultant's career.

# PREFACE

Often, however, the resultant accumulated pressure from dealing with these issues over the long term drives consultants out of the profession.

Although this book reflects my own views and experiences, I've canvassed a number of my colleagues who have generously given their permission to be quoted. I selected each of these consultants because of their professionalism, contribution to the profession, and longevity in the profession. They have supported themselves as consultants over the long haul and reflect a variety of specialties, organizational structures, and geographic locations. I have a great deal of respect for them and their families, all of whom I've been privileged to get to know. A successful consultant needs and acknowledges the support his or her family provides through the business cycles and the physical and emotional demands made. And each of these consultants characterizes success: they make money and make a positive difference for their clients by doing high-quality work.

Singling out only a few consultants from the thousands I've met is hard, but space limitations make it impossible to name all those I've met and who have made a difference for me. I've selected those I've quoted extensively, thus indicating how much of an effect they've had on *my* career.

Gary Goldstick became a consultant specializing in turnarounds fifteen years ago after learning his lesson as CEO of his own engineering company. Gary has published a number of books and spoken at many conferences. He likes to relate that he learned from making every mistake possible, yet his success shows that he is an excellent student and an even better teacher and coach. He has been able to transform his experience into wisdom.

Ira Gottfried has been the premier management consultant specializing in data processing in southern California for many decades. He has been a mentor, personal friend, and neighbor who has

# PREFACE

always made time for me and many other consultants as we learned our lessons. He took his consultancy to such a pinnacle of professionalism and competency that it was bought in its entirety by one of the Big Six firms. He has retired twice, and may well do so many more times. He has spoken and written extensively on all aspects of consulting as a business and has given his time and expertise to his community and his profession.

Bob Kahn is synonymous with ethics in consulting. A retail specialist who has also been an officer of consulting organizations in the United States, Bob has managed to pursue nationwide consulting and equally intense community involvement over six decades. He has combined an informal personal approach with extreme professionalism in service delivery.

I met Jack Schroeder fifteen years ago when I was consulting with his employer, a large engineering company in southern California. Jack was interested in moving out of the executive room into the consultant's rat race. Doing everything right, Jack became a respected consultant who has given back to the consulting profession in so many ways: as a speaker, as an officer, and as president of the local chapter of the Institute of Management Consultants and of other organizations. He gives 150 percent to his clients, who value his competence and professionalism.

Mickey Rosenau recently moved to Houston after decades in southern California. Perhaps he has taught us all he could and now seeks greener consultants to bring along. The most organized professional I've had the pleasure to meet, Mickey has been active in a number of professional and charitable organizations nationwide and within the community. Mickey writes extensively and is a well-known producer and deliverer of seminars. An engineer by training and an executive by experience, he distills these two disciplines into a client delivery system marked by ethics and professionalism of the highest nature.

## PREFACE

Maybe Mickey left southern California to be nearer to Ed Stone, president of the Dallas Marketing Group. Ed, a past president and officer of consulting organizations, has led his successful company for many years. He travels extensively for his clients and has a notable number of repeat clients—the clear sign of good work performed consistently.

Somers White, a former Arizona senator, has contributed to the consulting profession in his area of expertise, to the benefit of many consultants who have been able to sit at the foot of this professional Socrates. Somers has refused to allow consultants to get by with their technical competence alone; he has raised the consciousness and abilities of many of us with his tips for professional delivery and salesmanship. Many consultants initially were taken aback by his open discussion of sales and our personal delivery, but he speaks only to crowded rooms, and many consultants discreetly make the trip to Phoenix to seek out his counsel.

The thread noted in each of these successful consultants is their commitment to the profession; a high ethical standard; longevity as a consulting business; their assistance to others in the profession; and, for most, a technical background and hands-on experience at some point during their previous (before consulting) lives. They also share a strong and understanding support system; each has a spouse who has endured the years of overwork, stress, insecurity, and volatility while providing a support system without which consultants often lose their way.

Management consulting is not for everyone. But for those few with the energy, wit, wisdom, and psychological composition, management consulting can prove to be the most exciting manner of earning a livelihood. I've been doing it for more than two decades and have found it to be an exhilarating profession and a fulfilling experience. It is, at its best, never dull. It is, at its worst, never boring. It is what I have chosen and continue to choose to do with the rest of my life because making a positive difference in the lives of others is the backbone of my personal life strategy.

If reading this book makes a difference in the life of you, the reader, then I am fulfilled.

MARSHA D. LEWIN, FCMC

*Los Angeles, California*
*August 1995*

# ACKNOWLEDGMENTS

This book is a compilation of lessons learned and lessons taught. It could not have been written without my friends and mentors. Every consultant with whom I came in contact over the years taught me, overtly and by example. Each client contributed to the experience reflected in this book. These special folks are too numerous to cite individually, but each knows who he or she is. Forgive me for not mentioning each name, but thank you deeply.

Particularly, I am indebted to my mentors: Jim Kennedy, Ira Gottfried, Keith Kennedy, and Mickey Rosenau whose coaching, counsel and friendship helped me to articulate my concepts more clearly—to Jim for his guidance; to Ira for his encouragement; to Keith for his example; and to Mickey for his ideals.

My thanks go to the Wiley staff, who provided the practical guidance and help that make dreams become reality: to Mary Daniello, my attentive and helpful managing editor; to Bernice Pettinatto, who did a superb job editing the copy; to Giorgetta McRee, the

# ACKNOWLEDGMENTS

designer; to Susan Sinnott and Nicole Nowitz, the assistants who followed through the nits and crises; especially to Missy Garnett, the project manager who held everything together when we reached production; with great warmth and affection, to Ruth Mills, whose encouragement and attentiveness spanned the continent and whose contributions improved this effort greatly; and to Vito Tanzi, who told Ruth about me and my passion for consulting, and enabled me to meet the editor every writer dreams of but seldom meets.

Finally, I wish to acknowledge these folks, lest I be remiss: my wonderful friends, who have patiently endured my cycles of feast and famine, and have outwaited my unavailability; Maxine McCarty, whose mastery of technology, managing a consulting practice office, and of me, are greatly treasured; and my son David, who has taught me much about human nature, without which nothing else would have been possible.

M.D.L.

# CONTENTS

# CONTENTS

## PART TWO

## The Business of Management Consulting:
## Is This Really How You Want to Spend Tomorrow?

# CONTENTS

# CONTENTS

# CONTENTS

## PART THREE

## Survival Issues in Consulting: Is This Really How You Want to Spend Your Life?

# CONTENTS

# LIST OF EXHIBITS

# LIST OF EXHIBITS

## PART ONE

# Getting Started

## Is This How You Really Want to Spend Tonight?

# CHAPTER 1

---

# Some Fundamental Realities of Becoming a Consultant

**W**elcome! Presumably you could be watching television this evening but have chosen to read this book instead. Maybe you were let go by your employer today; perhaps you've just had it with the office political struggles; or perhaps you've had an offer to work as a consultant rather than as an employee. Well, before you jump from the security of what you do know, you should understand a bit more about the consulting profession.

## SEPARATING FACT FROM FANTASY

The best thing about dreams is that you never have to deal with the reality of reality. While you have sat cooped up in your noisy office, you've been daydreaming about leaving and parlaying your expertise into a small consulting practice that will allow you to come and go where and when you choose; allow you to pick your clients; and pay you handsomely for your expertise and interpersonal skills.

Closer to the truth, however, is that you are about to run a business, with yourself as the product sold. You are always on. Unless you have someone selling you, you must doff and don marketing, production, and administrative hats while remaining unobserved by the client. You must be confident (but not cocky); dignified (but not stuffy); technologically competent (but not a techie); sensitive (but not emotional); assertive (but not dominating); and the list goes on and on. The Delphic Oracle probably had an easier time of it than you may have as you venture out into the consulting world.

## TYPES OF CONSULTANTS

There are many definitions of management consulting; I've always best liked that used by a mentor and dear friend, Ira Gottfried, who says that a management consultant is "a person who himself has been in management and works only with the top and middle management of corporations on specific business-related assignments." I distinguish carefully between management consultants and other consultants, who address their specific range of services to other organizational levels within the company.

## WAYS TO PRACTICE

You can work for yourself, with a partner, or as part of a consultant organization. As a singleton (solo), you have freedom of action and decision but must assume all of the risk. You have no one with whom to share the overhead costs, such as telephone, advertising, and secretarial help. If you've come from an environment steeped in political cabals, this may seem to be the best alternative when you strike out as a consultant.

As a doubleton (with a partner), you can share the overhead costs but then have to reconcile issues such as unequal revenues brought into the practice, inequalities in use of resources, and the thousands of irritations that cause partnerships to dissolve regularly. A lethal combination results when two or more consultants, none of whom draws a particularly large audience or client base, group together to form a company tagged with a name that connects to none of the principals. Without overt market draw, the group has to create name recognition, having lost any familiarity potential clients might have had with the individual names. Resolution of the issues of cost versus benefits gained can often be brutal.

If you really enjoy working for a company with name recognition and more formal working hours and promotion paths, striking out on your own may lead you further from your goal. You might do well to consider joining one of the large firms (the Big Six) that offer management consulting as one of many specialties that might also include auditing and accounting. The overhead types of considerations such as bookkeeping, withholding taxes, secretarial service, insurance benefits, and marketing are generally assumed by the larger firms, and you can spend your time consulting and generating more consulting business.

Chapter 3 discusses the business form issue in more detail. Regardless of the organizational form you decide upon, however, the one thing you should be aware of is that a management consultant must sell, sell, and continue to sell. If your first reaction to that is "Not me," then maybe you should return tomorrow to your current situation and start counting rather than cursing your blessings.

# GENERALIST VS. SPECIALIST

The best way to decide you're getting into the right profession before making some hard-to-live-with commitments is to do an informal skills inventory. List your experience and talents by industry and by function. Then highlight those activities you really enjoy. For example, although I have written many policies and procedures manuals for client companies over the years, I don't enjoy that activity nearly as much as designing a system of procedures and automated tools to enable the company to gain and sustain market share. I prefer activities that bring me to people individually, such as management coaching, rather than teaching in the group environment. My lists looked like Exhibit 1-1, separated by function and by industry.

I also recommend looking at the various business development and management tasks you'll have to perform if you want to become a solo management consultant and rate those tasks according to how much you enjoy them. Exhibit 1-2 provides an example. (You may want to complete this chart after you've read Part Two.) If you don't enjoy keeping your own accounting records, doing your client billings, and marketing your services, you can hire someone to perform those functions for you—but you need to generate enough fees to cover their salaries.

If you look at your lists and have an industry focus—or a technical specialty that allows you to serve various professions and industries—then you can consider yourself a specialist. If you have a potpourri of clients and functions served, then you are probably a generalist, serving to bring the experience and perspective of many different functions into a business. Probably you serve smaller businesses if you are a generalist.

It's usually easier to market a specialty because the more precise you can be in your services, the easier it is to attract the attention

**Exhibit 1-1**

SKILLS INVENTORY

| Tasks | Industry | Function | Enjoy Most |
|---|---|---|---|
| Project management | Construction | Project director | * |
| Program specifications | Multiple | Design, document | |
| Interim management | Engineering | Division manager | * |
| Strategic planning | Multiple | Team leader, facilitator | |
| Management coaching | Multiple | Seminar leader | |
| Define standards | Multiple | Define policies and procedures | |
| Turnaround management | Multiple | Alter staff, increase productivity | * |
| Perform requirements analysis | Produce distribution | Design, document | |
| Strategic technology plan | Construction | Design, validate | |

of the audience. For example, when I started out, my card read, "Specializing in data processing for the stock brokerage industry." Specializing works beautifully as long as there are enough potential clients in the market segment to keep you busy. But with all specialties, time catches up, so you will need to keep updating your knowl-

# GETTING STARTED

**Exhibit 1-2**

TASK PREFERENCES RATING CHART

| Business Task | Like | Accept | Dislike |
|---|---|---|---|
| Sales/proposals | | | |
| Marketing | | | |
| Managing others | | | |
| Accounting | | | |
| Administration | | | |
| Planning | | | |
| Public relations | | | |
| Contract negotiation | | | |
| Accounts payable | | | |
| Accounts receivable | | | |
| Legal | | | |
| Task performance (e.g., design, evaluation) | | | |

edge and possibly even changing your marketplace. Beware of the business card that says "specializing in . . ." followed by a list of five or six items. No one can know everything about that many items, and the image this listing presents to a potential client is unfocused. (If you absolutely *must* specialize in multiple items, print separate business cards for each unrelated specialty, and use them appropriately.)

Another word of caution about specializing: There are fads within management consulting, as there are within the economy in general. Yogurt stores and software shops have flourished and expired, and so have industrial engineers, executive recruiters, and management information systems professionals. At certain times, there were many consultants in those areas, who ultimately closed up shop when the fad had passed. If you are going to be a faddish specialist, consider what is going to distinguish you from competing consultants.

## SELLING YOURSELF

The most common mistake I've observed over the years in new (and some established) consultants is the presumption that the world will beat a path to your door as soon as you hang out your shingle. Often the easiest assignment to get is the first one, which may be from your current employer. But after that, going out and knocking on doors or calling with a cheery good morning just isn't comfortable for many consultants. Perhaps it's an intellectual holdover from the view that professional services should not have to be marketed because the clarity and brilliance of their content are worthy enough to generate unending clients.

If you, as a potential new consultant, can don your prospective client's hat for a moment and ask yourself why she or he should hire you over competitors, you might get a better understanding of the dilemma the client faces when trying to select. It's hard to view the qualities of a consultant, especially in the soft specialties (such as corporate culture and participative process consulting) where the process is more important than the task.

Repeatedly I've heard CEOs and users of consultants comment that they do not select their consultants from the Yellow Pages; they prefer word-of-mouth referrals from peers. So the dilemma the new consultant faces is getting his or her name in front of the client with a personal recommendation attached. Cold calls and brochures alone are not going to make it.

## SUMMARY

By this point you have probably decided you're going through with this effort, and you've made decisions on whether you will work alone or with someone else, whether you will be an industry or functional specialist or a generalist, and whether management consulting is even what you want to do. Now you're ready to embark on your new career: successfully selling yourself and performing assignments for satisfied clients. Let's start with your first assignment.

# CHAPTER 2

# Getting Started

There are really no barriers to entry (or to exit) in the consulting profession. Unlike medicine, which requires a rigorous education and certification process, management consultants can draw upon their experience and knowledge and be successful in the profession. As a result, many individuals enter the profession who lack the business skills and, especially, the communication skills to become truly successful consultants. They leave in their wake unhappy and unsatisfied clients, who then view all consultants as charlatans rather than as professionals.

Education is an important component of any profession, and formalizing the experience we have into a presentable, comprehensible body of knowledge is important. There are three ways of obtaining that knowledge:

1. Academically, through a curriculum specializing in management consulting practice.
2. Professionally, through local and national groups with programs culminating in a certification designation.
3. Experientially, by on-the-job training rendering you an expert in a specific field.

Of course, you won't have time to go through an academic curriculum to be credentialed or through an association's accrediting process if you want to become a consultant soon. But if you've been thinking of consulting, you must feel that you have a salable expertise in an area that your future clients will generally want to buy. Your education thus far has probably been through the baptism by fire that creates expertise. And probably you already have your expertise, although you might want to contact local and national associations specializing in disseminating that body of knowledge and those principles (see the appendix at the end of the book). Since most of these organizations have local or regional activities, you can get the names of local contacts, and if you do embark on consulting, attend local meetings where you can meet other consultants who can mentor you through the process. (This type of education is generally more valuable for new consultants with industry experience.)

The immediate task tonight is to get you ready to start an assignment as soon as possible. You will need a business name—and, in fact, your own name is often the simplest way to start. You won't have to do corporate searches in all the states in which you wish to do business to see if somebody is already using a name, and you can start quickly.

# THE WET BUSINESS CARD

All consultants must have business cards—to accompany the power suit and serious shoes, of course. The first decision should be to get your stationery and cards printed. Simple stationery on the best paper you can obtain is always the best choice. You can develop your corporate logo and engrave your stationery after you've been in business for a while; this is just to bootstrap you for the moment. If you're unsure about the possible image you might be creating, look at this as your first such purchase, to be followed by the real stuff once you get going. Today, with laser printers and local printing stores able to turn out professional-quality cards and stationery quickly and at reasonable cost, you can create a simple but professional image for yourself overnight.

My image progressed over a quarter century of practice from a first business card on inexpensive white stock, in e.e. cummings style—see Exhibit 2-1. Later I merely used my own name (in the same font, to maintain some continuity) and then changed to **Lewin Associates** (still in black on white paper but with a somewhat differ-

**Exhibit 2-1**
BASIC BUSINESS CARD

| | |
|---|---|
| **marsha d. lewin & associates** | **marsha d. lewin** |
| | consultant to management |
| 12119 inavale place | |
| los angeles, california 90049 | 213-472-0825 |
| specializing in data processing for the stock brokerage industry | |

**Exhibit 2-2**
A MORE SOPHISTICATED BUSINESS CARD

**Marsha D. Lewin, CDP, CSP, FCMC**
President

**Marsha D. Lewin Associates, Inc.**
Consultants to Management
P.O. Box 641277
Los Angeles, CA 90064
Phone: 310-446-8833
Fax:    310-446-8834
Internet: 72622.3112@compuserve.com

ent font). Only in 1984 did I go to a professional public relations company, which designed a logo for me and an image. I still maintain the logo, which is blue, on a cream-colored expensive-weight card and with engraved cream stationery (see Exhibit 2-2). The logo appears on report covers I've had printed, as well as notecards used to confirm meetings, to enclose newspaper articles I've clipped out, and just to say hello. This is a much more expensive solution than I would recommend for your first venture into consulting, however.

# AND WHO ARE YOU?
# DEVELOPING A MARKETING BROCHURE

The general consensus is that having a brochure doesn't help you, but not having one will hurt you. A corollary is that having a poor one will hurt you, while having a good one won't help you. It's a conundrum of the first order. Given laser printers and word processing, the best choice is to generate a brief statement of what you do, your experience, and perhaps how you conduct an assignment. Print it so that you can fold it into thirds; and, voilà! there is a foldout brochure to insert into your newly printed envelopes with a cover letter. Local printing stores carry an assortment of laser-ready brochure paper, or you can order some from any number of mail-order stationery companies. This paper tends to be heavier and often comes with discreetly colored borders to enrich your look. Again, make sure the brochure represents you well in terms of content and presentation. I think we consultants often forget to include the sizzle in our brochures, trading off sparkle for image, but that's an individual preference.

I have a variety of brochures for my business at the moment: a small piece that gives a quick overview of what I do and how I can assist a potential client, and word-processed larger company descriptions that are customized for particular industries in which I have noteworthy experience. I send the small brochure out whenever possible; its size and light weight make it inexpensive and convenient. The large brochures go out only in response to requests for detailed information on my company and specific resources and assignments we provide. It is an extensive document, which I found costly to send to everyone and, most important, overwhelming.

I confess that I seldom send out these brochures, with our company report covers, because I've finally understood *the principle of waning attention*: If it takes longer than 3 seconds to make a potential client aware of what you can do, you'll never get the chance to do it for that person. Thus, the best brochure for you will be brief, expressed in terms of what benefits the client can obtain from your services, with lots of white space so that he or she can quickly read it. If it takes too long to read, or appears too wordy or too imprecise, your materials will end up as recycled matter.

My current brochure is reproduced in Exhibit 2-3. It tells what

**Exhibit 2-3**

SAMPLE MARKETING BROCHURE

# The Answer

# To Your

# Questions . . .

**Marsha D. Lewin Associates**
**Consultants to Management**

## WHAT WE DO

*We sit down with you and your key people and determine how you really do business.* This interviewing process also gives us an opportunity to identify your internal resources whose participation in the effort will reduce your costs and leave you with valuable in-house knowledge. We also gather changes you'd like to see implemented.

*We identify growth issues* for you so that, for example, your computer system will be able to communicate with the new divisions and companies you plan.

*We canvass the hardware and software vendors* specializing in your industry or profession, for your size of company now – and where you want it to be.

*We've been around long enough to separate out marketing hype from true capabilities.* We know how to recommend a system that can grow modularly as your company grows, yet still be cost-effective now. We know this from our own experience, not from texts. We've been doing this long enough to state that *the business problems are always people problems;* the technology can always be made to serve your needs.

*We negotiate with vendors.* We are not affiliated with any particular vendor, although we like certain hardware and software products because of their service and customer receptiveness. We try to save you money by buying necessary components only, by up-front negotiations to prevent later dissatisfaction, and by matching your expectations with reality. Vendors tend to respond more to us since we may not recommend future clients to them; your leverage is limited because you are only buying a single system a single time.

*We know what is needed* to phase the new systems and procedures into your environment. Sometimes it's a new computer and storage facility; sometimes new labor talents: data entry, computer operations, facilities management, programming, systems analysis, technical documentation.

*We can provide you the capability* on a short term basis while you go through your conversion and testing, or help you in hiring and training your own personnel. Our goal is to leave you self-sufficient, not reliant upon the consultant organization.

*We plan the conversion for you:* how and when it will take place, who will participate, and what constitutes acceptance.

*We document for, and train, your staff.* We set up procedures for them to follow that will ensure the necessary continuity and stability of your systems – and associated procedures.

*We serve as architects* – we design an overall business structure; we then "architect"

16

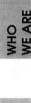

an information system whose structure supports your special business structure. We are also engineers: we "engineer" the proper solution to best suit your needs using contemporary tools and management concepts.

*We can design and implement special management applications for you* – to supplement your purchased software products or to facilitate your procedures. We are not to be confused with contract programmers, although we do provide programming services for our clients who do not want to have a technical support staff to nurture (and pay) after the completion of the system implementation.

*We manage your operation:* particularly in the startup mode – but occasionally in a transition mode, such as a departing manager; the need for a manager to bridge into a new operational mode; or to effect a turnaround in a company or division that has lost sight of its charter. We are not limited merely to data processing management; we have managed operations for many companies at the divisional level. Both require quick decision-making based on quantifiable and qualitative information!

*We go away!* To everything there is a season; when our work with you is done, we leave. We're always available if you need us again, but we won't stay longer than needed to finish the job.

# WHO WE ARE

We provide counsel to businesses in the implementation of computer systems into their corporations, and the optimization of existing technology. If this were an easy task, then surely businesses would be acquiring computer financial and information systems in the same way they buy their copiers and fax machines. However, the computer is only a small part of what is being acquired; the operative word really is *system*.

A system ties together people, diverse needs, management styles, and procedures. Businesspeople who try to save some money may find that they've been shortsighted: they can possibly avert disaster by taking the corrective action themselves, but may end up destroying the system and its data, or only using a tiny portion of the system's capabilities.

Time and again, Marsha D. Lewin Associates has saved clients money and effort, producing excellent results at a cost below that which a "do-it-yourself" approach really costs.

# Marsha D. Lewin Associates
## Consultants to Management

## Marsha D. Lewin

As president of Marsha D. Lewin Associates, a management consulting firm specializing in project management and information system implementation, Marsha Lewin has managed, designed and implemented many information systems for businesses.

Recent representative assignments have included: interim division and project management; corporate management information requirements analysis; computer hardware and software evaluation; selection and contract negotiation; micro/mainframe computer network implementation; user and technical training; feasibility studies; management coaching; and system design.

Ms. Lewin holds an AB degree from Barnard College, a Master of Science degree in Computer Science, *summa cum laude,* from West Coast University and a Master of Business Administration degree from Pepperdine University's Presidential/Key Executive (PKE) Program. She is a Certified Management Consultant (CMC), holds the Certificate in Data Processing (CDP), and is a Certified Systems Professional (CSP).

She is an active member and former officer of a number of professional and civic organizations including the Board of Directors of the West Coast University Alumni Association, and nationally, the Institute of Management Consultants, the Construction Management Association of America, and the Council of Consulting Organizations.

Co-author of the book, *Software Project Management Step by Step,* and author of many articles, Ms. Lewin is also a featured instructor on project and related management topics in live seminars, educational video and audio tapes. She is included in *Who's Who* volumes that list American Business Leaders, American Finance and Industry, American Women, and the Computer Industry.

17

we do, who we are, and who I am. I use my picture because it adds another dimension to the brochure, breaking up the verbiage. However, it required professional photographs, which take time and money, and the brochure must be updated periodicially lest a potential client mistake me, as I age, for my daughter! Our image must reflect who we are, not merely who we have been!

Answering the following questions will provide you with enough initial information to produce a simple but effective fold-over brochure.

## Who Are You and What Do You Do?

> J. J. Jones Consulting specializes in reducing postconstruction claims through the application of proven automated tools to construction phase procedures.

If the reader is not in a construction-related field, the initial statement defining the service provided will fall on deaf ears. On the other hand, I generally want my initial assignment to be within my comfortable sphere of operations.

A brief, concise statement is often referred to as the "elevator speech"; every successful consultant I know has mastered it. If you are lucky enough to find yourself in an elevator with your prime marketing target and you've got three floors of time in which to explain what you do to pique his or her interest, what would you say? After many years, I've managed to state mine in this way: "We provide to the design/build professions management consulting services which reduce risk by increasing automated controls."

## What Specific Services Do You Offer?

Now you can tell what you do: a set of perhaps 6 points that identify the tasks you perform in executing an assignment—but in client terms. Here are a few examples:

"I develop a marketing strategy based on the changes in your company and industry."
"I enable you to bring new products rapidly to market before your competition."
"I design warehouses customized to your distribution and product requirements."

## Can You Tell Me What You've Done in the Past That Would Be Applicable?

If you don't have a prior client list, prepare a list of assignments you've done for previous employers—for example:

"Increased productivity in a hand-tools distribution company by 15 percent."
"Reduced receivables in a food processing company by $2 million through implementation of a customized accounting system."

Quantify results wherever you can. "I made things function better" is hardly enough for someone to understand what you really can do.

## Who Did You Do This For?

List your client and employer names. You don't have to indicate your status (employee or consultant) when you performed each task, but be sure that you can produce a person at each company listed as a favorable reference if you have to.

19

## Who Are You?

Provide a brief description of your background, educational and professional, as well as a few interesting things about yourself. For example, I have many academic degrees and certifications and an unusually heavy history of involvement in professional organizations. But when I include some reference to my past experience as a soccer player, I often generate interest that results in a call I might not have otherwise gotten.

# GETTING THAT FIRST ASSIGNMENT: GOING FISHING

Presumably the printer is busily working on your cards and stationery, you've got the brochure ready for reproduction, and now you need to determine the beneficiaries of your enlightened experience. My suggestion is that you sit down with a large pad of lined paper, and start identifying all the folks you know who are in industries or companies that may need your services. This is the first step in the development of your "Good People" list, the mainstay of a consultant's business development effort. Criteria for inclusion include anyone you have met and will remember you who:

- Works in a company/industry you've targeted.
- Has contacts personally or professionally that may be useful.
- "Owes you one" (the Godfather certainly knew what he was doing!).

There are many wonderful and comprehensive books on the marketing of consulting services (the Bibliography at the end of this book lists a few), and there's no reason to repeat the sage advice in those tomes.

You can now send letters announcing your new consulting practice (announcement cards are even classier) to the folks on your

Good People list, and follow the mailing up with telephone calls to arrange a visit. The purpose of many of these calls and visits is merely to get the name of another individual within the targeted organization or profession who might have more information on who is hiring consultants, and for what tasks. Your goal is to get to the individual who allocates the funds—hopefully to you.

Be sure to follow up each meeting with a thank-you note to your Good People for the referral; it's a nice touch that keeps your name and good manners in front of them. In fact, a trick I learned from one of my mentors is to send one of our "compliments" cards to confirm the appointment and then follow the actual meeting with a note on our letterhead or, if I promised to remit something, another compliments card as the transmittal. Our compliments card is small but professional looking; see Exhibit 2-4 for a sample.

Working your Good People list is extremely effective. Recently I had a call from a woman who had left her defense-related employment after decades of extensive experience in cost reduction. Because the southern California business landscape has been so dreadful, she was uncomfortable calling former associates to see if they knew of opportunities for her. After encouragement, she started making calls and discovered that her former coworkers, now scattered among many other companies, were delighted to hear from her and reestablish contact and anxious to assist her move back into the world as a consultant. They remembered her as a conscientious and reliable individual whose talents could be applied in their new companies.

## GETTING A NIBBLE: ASSESSING A POTENTIAL ASSIGNMENT

After chumming around for a while, you should end up with a likely prospect or two. If you were one of the fortunate who was offered

**Exhibit 2-4**

SAMPLE "WITH COMPLIMENTS" CARD

**Marsha D. Lewin Associates**  Consultants to Management

*With compliments*

P.O. Box 641277
Los Angeles, CA 90064
Phone: 310-446-8833 Fax: 310-446-8834

a consulting assignment before you left your previous situation, then you've just averted the toughest part of the entry into the icy waters of consulting.

Presumably the client is interested in your services for a specific task, and you have impressed this person with your qualifications and ability to perform that task. Now the hard discussions are to take place:

- Who is your competition?
- What will it take to get the client to award the assignment to you?
- What fees are involved?

The greatest danger at this point is that you will lose the client by not asking the questions that are crucial to you as a consultant. For example, failing to ask who the competition is can result in your spending endless amounts of time generating a proposal that is not going to measure up to that of a Big Six accounting firm, or it may reveal previous affiliations with consultants that may well result in your being overlooked in the award process.

After many decades in consulting, I'm still reluctant to ask prospects what they need from me for us to win the assignment. But when I muster up the courage to ask directly, I often am blessed with an equally direct answer.

I view any assignment as having three dimensions: schedule, cost, and scope. Sometimes the *schedule* is the most important factor: An assignment must be completed within such stringent time limits that cost and job scope are less critical, and the client will settle for a report that is not bound and footnoted and is willing to pay more to have the schedule met. For example, on our assignment to develop construction monitoring systems for the reactivation/ modernization of the battleship *Missouri*, implementing the control systems was time critical. If the information monitoring the construction status was not available before the ship had to go to sea, our mission would have failed, regardless of how well the information was presented or how little it cost.

Sometimes *cost* is the most important factor: The client doesn't have much money, so the task has to be cut back to fit the budget. This is often the case with small companies, which prefer to have a consultant implement the recommendations but lack the financial resources to do so.

And sometimes *performance* is the most important factor: It doesn't matter how much it costs or how long it takes, but the performance of what is delivered is paramount. For example, products designed for the space shuttle have to be perfect; anything less results in failure of the entire mission.

Once you know which dimension is most important to the client, you can configure a proposal of work geared toward the client's needs, thus increasing your chances of landing the assignment.

Sometimes, though, you should walk away from an assignment that doesn't feel right for any one or more of the following reasons:

- The money is too small for the scope being requested.
- The task isn't one you're experienced at.
- You don't like the client (chemistry is missing).
- You don't understand what they're asking for and what they want to do.
- You don't have the time to do it properly.

## BAITING THE HOOK: PREPARING A PROPOSAL AND SETTING YOUR FEE

Once you've found a potential client, he or she may ask you to submit a formal proposal for the work you'll perform. Again, the technique of proposal writing has been addressed in many superb books, so I won't address that here (see Chapter 6 and the Bibliography for a brief list). But you should be aware that despite a Request for Proposal (RFP), not all proposals are really desired or considered. My experience is that many companies themselves are on fishing trips: They are looking for free advice, and after they have surveyed a group of consultants, they find they are sufficiently educated to use the templates provided by the better proposals to attempt to perform the task themselves. Sometimes they fail abjectly; at other times, we have done such a good job of explaining what we do and how that the client can do it without us!

With respect to fees, often it is truly impossible to estimate accurately the costs of an assignment at the outset. When this happens, I break the assignment into phases, so that the client can decide whether it's worth going on with the next phase and I can better calibrate how long it will take me to accomplish tasks in the client's environment.

In my field, I have made a tactical decision not to perform fixed-price work. If we take less time, the client benefits from the reduced fees; if it takes more time, we are adequately compensated for our work. Especially if you are just starting out, I advise doing time and materials assignments, since you may not yet know what it takes to get a task accomplished in an organization in which you have no line authority. "Time and materials" is a fee basis where you bill the client for the time you put in (hours or days multiplied by an agreed-upon rate) plus any materials directly chargeable to the assignment (e.g., direct costs such as phone, mileage, reproduction). You can reduce your client's discomfort by giving a "not to exceed" figure and ensuring that you monitor the fees charged to date as you conduct the assignment.

Recently, I violated my fixed-price decision and took on a very large public sector assignment with another consultant and a team of people, most of whom I had worked with on past assignments. Since many of the unknowns were reduced in scoping out the assignment and we had worked for the client on two phases immediately preceding this award, I felt we could estimate the true costs of the assignment. The client achieved a fairer price because we were able to reduce risk.

Every proposal is different, depending on the client, the task, and your specialty. Nevertheless, the following issues come up every time you submit a proposal:

- *Background and definition of problem:* What caused the client to request your proposal and what business problem is going to be solved by your work.
- *Scope of the assignment you propose:* What you will do to solve the problem—and this means stating what you will *not* be doing.
- *How you will be doing it:* How the assignment will be conducted (with some specific information but in as general terms as possible so the client understands but can't do it without you); how frequently and in what manner status will be reported.
- *Deliverables:* What you will be producing during the course of your assignment (plans, seminars, programs, or designs) and who retains ownership of these.
- *Fees and costs:* Your estimate of how much the client can expect to pay, broken down into fees and reimbursable expenses identified as to class—for example, "Fees are estimated not to exceed $50,000, and reimbursable expenses are estimated at $8,000 (travel, telephone, materials, reproduction, express delivery)."
- *Resources needed:* On-site desk space, access to certain materials or individuals; specific personnel resources and the roles they are to play; on-site computer or other technology and equipment.
- *Schedule:* When you can start and when you expect the assignment to be completed if started on time; how long the fees proposed are in effect.

Chapter 6 provides more detailed information on how to write an effective proposal.

# REELING IT IN: WRITING THE CONTRACT

In the excitement of being awarded the assignment, don't forget to take care of the basics: Put the assignment scope and conditions in writing, *no matter how small the assignment!* Trust goes quite far while it exists, but after it has died, it seldom can be resuscitated. Over the years I've seen many legal documents and agreements used by consultants and their client companies, some quite lengthy and others brief. As long as the document is succinct and complete, you will protect both yourself and the client from misunderstandings.

I've used the format shown in Exhibit 2-5 successfully for many years on small and medium assignments without problems. It restates the proposal made to the prospective client. When working with larger public and private sector clients, however, I have to use their formats; they typically have their own legal departments with their own contracts, and those client forms take precedence. *However*, when using someone else's form, don't be penny-wise and pound foolish: Pass the agreement by a trusted lawyer to ensure that you are not placing yourself or your assets in jeopardy by signing a contract that is one-sided or ambiguous or, worst, illegal.

As a practical matter, I don't believe consultants can risk suing a client for nonpayment, even with a written agreement. But having such an agreement certainly precludes misunderstandings when new parties become involved (as when the manager is replaced in the middle of your assignment) and enables you to keep focused on why you were brought in.

By the way, if you are going to join up with someone else in performing your assignment, be sure to have a written agreement with him or her as well. This issue is covered in greater detail in Chapters 3 and 5. It should *not* be overlooked.

Exhibit 2-5
## SAMPLE LETTER OF AGREEMENT

This Letter of Agreement is a restatement of MDLA's proposal to Client Company's Officer of 10 April, 1995, with locations for our respective signatures, to constitute authorization to start work. Items such as status report and invoicing formats will be addressed in our meeting on July 17.

Parties:

Client Company
Marsha D. Lewin Associates, Inc. (MDLA)

Scope:

This Agreement covers Management Consulting Services to assist Client Company in its selection and implementation of an automated system to support its projected future growth and strategies.

We propose a five phased project for Client Company. Each phase is described below as to purpose, time required to accomplish it, and what deliverables you can expect to have from the phase. Each phase can be priced more precisely as one gets closer, when some of the prerequisite options have been selected. For example, one cannot exactly establish the cost of the implementation at this point because the vendor selected may provide services at no cost that others might charge you for.

*Phase I:*     **Determine Executive Requirements**

The purpose of this phase is to determine Client Company's long range plans, to ensure that the detailed requirements for the automated system selected support those plans. If a formal strategic plan and corpo-

**Exhibit 2-5**

CONTINUED

rate mission statement already exist in usable form, this phase can take as little as 5 hours or as many as 20 hours.

The deliverables from this phase should be a high-level 5–8 year strategy statement, as well as a corporate mission statement. Typically it is presented in brief, bulletized format.

*Phase II:*    **Determine User and Functional Requirements**

The purpose of this phase is to determine, through interviews of selected managers and key personnel, the features that a new system must possess, as well as those features which are desirable but not mandatory.

The deliverables from this phase are the Functional Requirements Document, which can be used as the basis for a subsequent Request for Proposal (RFP); an evaluation of the existing hardware, software, and personnel resources that comprise your current technical support; and a set of recommendations that might reap some short-term benefits for you, regardless of which vendor or option is ultimately selected.

Access to any background documents previously developed will be of great help.

This phase can take 20–50 hours, presuming 10 interviews and a written report.

*Phase III:*    **Determine Alternatives**

The purpose of this phase is to select and weigh various alternatives for Client Company: hardware platforms and software vendors; continu-

## Exhibit 2-5
## CONTINUED

ing with the current vendor; or some combination thereof. Depending upon the long-range strategy, these alternatives would include implementation in stages, to minimize capital outlays for equipment that might not be used initially; and to accommodate intervals for training personnel. A usual component of this phase is the solicitation of proposals from selected vendors to whom a prepared RFP has been circulated.

The deliverables from this phase can be: the RFP; a set of suggested architectures for comparative evaluation; the proposals submitted in response to the RFP; and ratings of these proposals.

The time required for this phase can be more accurately estimated during Phase II, when the functional requirements' scope is more clearly known, and the involvement of other consultants and staff has been clarified. Variables involved are the numbers of vendor demonstrations attended, the numbers of vendors solicited, and those responding to the RFP. Using 5 solicitations and 3 responses, a plausible figure would be 50 hours, plus 20 hours for technical evaluations of the responses.

*Phase IV:*  **Vendor Negotiation**

The purpose of this phase is to clarify any ambiguities between the proposal, Client Company's needs, and the vendor's contract, with the vendor (or vendor team) selected; and to negotiate the very best possible agreement at the best price attainable.

The deliverables from this phase are the signed contract, as well as a schedule of vendor deliverables, responsible parties, and the implementation schedule.

## Exhibit 2-5
## CONTINUED

The time required for this phase can be more accurately estimated during Phase II, when the contracted scope of work is more clearly known, and the involvement of other consultants and staff has been clarified. An estimate of 25 hours is submitted, subject to clarification.

*Phase V:* **Implementation**

The deliverables from this phase are a completely installed and functioning system, satisfying the stated executive strategic goals and the user functional requirements; a trained and self-sufficient staff able to operate and fully utilize the system as configured; and a set of usable technical and end-user documentation.

The time and consultant scope of involvement can be more accurately estimated during the preceding phase, according to the vendor contract(s) negotiated and the involvement of other consultants and Client Company's own staff. For initial estimating purposes, a 3-month implementation, utilizing 15 hours weekly (13 weeks) is suggested.

**Schedule**

The requirements analysis and executive strategic goals can be delivered within 6 weeks, depending upon availability of your staff for the requisite interviews. An initial target date would be September 15, given the executive planning session currently scheduled for July 24.

Subsequent milestones will be scheduled as the project progresses.

**Fees**

Fees currently in effect at MDLA are based upon labor category as follows. Direct costs, which typically on a project of this type include

## Exhibit 2-5
### CONTINUED

reproduction, messenger service, telephone, postage, and media, are billed at cost plus a 10% handling charge. If travel should be required, coach airfare plus normal travel expenses such as hotels, transportation, and meals would be included. Expenses other than these incidental expenses must be approved in advance by the client.

*Hourly Labor Rates*

| | |
|---|---|
| Senior Consultant | $150 |
| Accounting Specialist | $115 |
| Senior Database Analyst | $ 85 |
| Systems Programmer Analyst | $ 85 |
| Documentation Specialist | $ 60 |
| Administrative Analyst | $ 35 |

All travel time is charged at 50% of the applicable labor rate and 30 cents per mile. The minimum on-site billing charge is a half-day (4 hours).

### Personnel

I shall personally conduct the interviews and data gathering during Phases I and II, and shall be involved as architect and project manager throughout all phases. Wherever possible, I shall attempt to use your staff or our technical personnel when a cost savings can be achieved.

### Budget

The fees for these tasks, as estimated above, can be summarized by phase, as follows. Additional expenses, which include travel time and

## Exhibit 2-5
## CONTINUED

expenses, can be estimated at 18% of the fees, although this varies for each client assignment. The schedule and fees quoted assume the reasonable availability of Client Company's management and staff for interviews, data collection, and administrative tasks. Any changes in taskings and/or estimates will be documented and reported to Client Company's management as soon as apparent.

| Phase I: | $ 3,000 |
|----------|---------|
| Phase II: | $ 7,500 |
| Phase III: | $ 9,200 |
| Phase IV: | $ 3,750 |
| Phase V: | $19,500 |

## Invoicing

We submit invoices semi-monthly for services rendered during the applicable period, on the 15th and last day of each month. Invoices are payable upon presentation. Invoices unpaid within 30 days are subject to a 1% monthly interest fee.

## Term

The labor rates quoted above are protected for 6 months from the signature dates applicable to this Agreement.

## Confidentiality

We understand and respect our clients' needs for confidential treatment of their business issues and are sensitive to them. We shall keep your

## Exhibit 2-5
### CONTINUED

identity confidential when dealing with vendors to ensure your privacy until you indicate otherwise to us.

Again, we thank you for the opportunity to assist Client Company with this very interesting and important project. We are confident of our organization's ability to add value to your company through this effort.

Yours sincerely,


Marsha D. Lewin CDP CSP FCMC
President

MDL:gws

Approved for Client Company

Name: _____

Title: _____

Date: _____

---

# EYEBALL TO EYEBALL WITH YOUR NEW CLIENT

Whenever possible, present proposals, contractual documents, and reports, in person. Since you don't know the recipient's frame of mind when opening the envelope with your proposal, you might get a negative reaction rather than the favorable view you expected. Personally presenting the document(s) allows you to gauge the recipient's reaction and respond to it in such a way that she or he will hopefully be receptive to your ideas. A face-to-face meeting also increases the opportunity for previously unvoiced questions to be asked and for a relationship to develop between you and your prospective client.

Especially if you have bad news to deliver to a client—an employee who is not performing, a task that is going to be behind schedule despite everyone's best efforts, an unplanned-for expense that affects the budget—you should deliver it *personally on-site*, not over the telephone. Recently we selected a set of products for a client and in the process of prototyping them in the client environment discovered they did not interact as the vendors had promised. As we became more educated by working with the products, we asked additional questions of the references we had been given and discovered that there was dissatisfaction among existing users who had not voiced it because they had wanted a larger user base to help them out! I had to go to our client with an alternate plan, but spent the time to explain our fallback plan and the justifications. I could hardly have done this comfortably by telephone, fax, or letter and achieved the same client support.

## CONDUCTING THE ASSIGNMENT

Presumably you know what needs to be done, you know how to do it, and you go about doing just that. During the project, ensure that you have regularly scheduled status meetings on any task more than a week in duration. You can keep the client reassured that the project is proceeding according to plan and have an opportunity to discuss any anomalous situations that might have arisen. These meetings serve to help you to get to know your client better, and your client can develop that trust in you and your abilities that is crucial to long-term success.

I recommend submitting a brief, written status report as well. I've used the following format effectively with clients:

- *Tasks accomplished:* Those items we planned to do and have done within the period of this status report.
- *Tasks to be accomplished:* What we plan to do in the coming period and with whom and when, as appropriate.
- *Open issues needing resolution:* To highlight promised resources that are unavailable, needed decisions that are still pending, or a schedule that is in jeopardy.

This report gives the client a brief summary of project status and affords him or her the opportunity to rearrange priorities and close open issues in a timely manner. A sample report is shown in Exhibit 2-6.

The most successful consultants I've known treat the individuals within the client organization with respect and dignity and avoid getting personal when clashing personalities are unearthed. For someone just coming out of a corporate environment, where such conflicts may be commonplace, a word of advice here: In organizations where such conflicts exist, they can be construed as part of the manner in which business is conducted. Management might not like these conflicts but often tolerate and preferably ignore them when possible. Unless your specific consulting task is to deal with such issues, just tolerate them and conduct your assignment without getting involved. Clearly, if the conflict involves the consultant and resolution is required, the consultant is more likely to get axed than the individual employee(s).

**Exhibit 2-6**
SAMPLE STATUS REPORT

---

January 18, 1996

**To:**       Client Executive
**From:**     Marsha Lewin
**Subject:**  Periodic Status Report 7

*Tasks Accomplished*
1. Management meeting held for senior executives off-site 1/5–6. Report prepared and submitted separately.
2. Attended demonstration of new accounting system at Happy Promises vendor site.

*Tasks to Be Accomplished*
1. Two more vendor demonstrations planned for next week.
2. Prepare report evaluating products and present to management. Meeting tentatively planned for 1/30 on-site.

*Open Issues Needing Resolution*
1. Electrical subcontractor has not been on-site to prepare room for new equipment. An alternate plan is needed to avoid schedule delay.

---

# DON'T TELL FISH STORIES

One consultant I've known had an uncanny knack for making the client sound rather stupid: He'd always be announcing that he just landed an assignment to define an assignment or was getting paid to write a proposal to do more work. The client sounded as though he'd been suckered in, and perhaps he felt that way because this consultant rarely got the add-on assignment and had great difficulty keeping his practice together over the years.

The client relationship must be characterized by dignity—on both sides of the fees—if it is to be successful. I've walked away from few assignments, and when I did, it was due to that lack of respect and dignity. Also, you'll soon find yourself facing closed doors if you are indiscreet in what you reveal among competitors. It is apparent to even casual listeners that your loose tongue can next be describing their innards to others, and that's a risk they probably don't want to take. In today's business environment, such revelations may even be illegal, as more and more companies require consultants to sign nondisclosure agreements before an assignment can be conducted.


## GO FOR THE GOLD MEDAL

The most important aspect of any assignment is how well you do it. After all, you want this assignment to be so successful that you will be remembered well and can use people you've encountered here as future references. How many people remember Olympic team hopefuls in any category who didn't place? Other than figure skater Nancy Kerrigan, how many even remember the silver medalists? No, we remember swimmer Mark Spitz and track and field star Rafer Johnson. (Of course, we *do* remember Tonya Harding. Bad press lives on.)

When you work, do the very best that you can, because you cannot be a successful consultant without doing good work, no matter how good your salesmanship may be. How is good work defined? In simplest terms, you performed what your client asked of you, as agreed between you, to the best of your abilities, and to his or her satisfaction. Pragmatically, your client was so pleased with what you did that he or she would definitely hire you again.

# COMPLETING THE ASSIGNMENT

It ain't over until the fat lady sings, and that may be long after the original agreement has been supplemented by other tasks for the client. But as a consultant, it's important for you to be sensitive to the distinction between being a consultant and being an employee. Consultants, like fish, begin to lose their freshness as they stay on. You need to learn to prepare for the ending, to end, and to leave. On long assignments this separation can be very difficult; I've found it still saddens me greatly. But these separations are to the client's benefit, because reliance on consultants, while remunerative for us, is often debilitating for the client.

Prepare a wind-down plan, and discuss it with your client to ensure there are no questions unanswered and no open issues needing resolution. Where appropriate, identify staff who will be responsible for carrying on any remaining work. Often I add a "parting shots" report, which summarizes issues the client should address in the future, and suggests plans for dealing with those issues. These reports are brief, but they help clients to solve problems themselves because they were properly alerted. Often they result in my being called in for assistance in the future.

After you prepare your final report and final bill, you might want to add, as a nice touch, a letter of gratitude to the client mentioning specific employees whose support made the project successful. I've relished the praise and recognition such employees have received from their management, as did they.

# KEEPING IN TOUCH

Now that you've completed your first assignment with a firm, don't forget the people there. Add to your Good People list the pivotal individuals you became acquainted with on the assignment and follow up by sending them articles you feel may be of interest. Every few months, take time for a business meal with the client (I prefer breakfast meetings, since Los Angeles is so large that it takes too long to get back and forth to client sites during the lunch hour). You'd be surprised at the repeat business that can be generated from a satisfied client, as well as information you might hear on industry trends or future opportunities.

# KEEPING YOUR HEAD ABOVE WATER

There is a marked tendency for consultants to become so immersed in a client assignment that they forget to come up for air for the duration. They forsake all contacts with peers and potential and past clients while the assignment is conducted. They might be able to focus on the issues at hand, but they may find huge peaks and valleys in their income stream. The consulting cycle becomes the conducting of assignments, followed by intense periods of marketing, then submersion again into the assignment process.

Most senior consultants who have made it in the profession believe *marketing is the most important and constant task the consultant must perform*, even when involved in a client assignment. Guidelines propose 20 percent time in marketing, or at least one day a week. I recommend at least one event, usually a meal, with someone not related to your client assignment, plus five telephone calls. The calls may not be easy if you end up spending considerable amounts of time at a client site, where telephones and privacy are not readily available. But it can be done, and should be done, if you want to keep the revenue coming in.

I confess to violating the guidelines and rules on a regular basis and suffering the consequences. Partly because I take on intensive full-time assignments with on-site requirements and partly because I take on nonlocal assignments, I end up unable to maintain face-to-face contact as I'd like. But I do try to keep telephone contacts up until I am geographically and physically able to get together with my network.

## YOU BE THE JUDGE

You've gone through that initial assignment, landing it with lesser or greater degrees of difficulty. You've gotten your business cards, stationery, and letters of agreement. You've been able to write a winning proposal, set your fees, sign a credible letter of agreement with your client, and conduct a successful assignment. You've gotten paid, hopefully, and have sustained your contacts so that you're ready for additional assignments. So how do you know if you're successful?

Unless you are working in a large firm as a consultant, the measure of your success as a management consultant is self-determined. You are the only one who can evaluate whether you've made a difference for the client; whether you've given all that you could to the client during the course of the assignment; and whether, in your opinion, the client got his or her money's worth.

As a solo practitioner, the odds are that no one will ever ask to check your timesheets; only you know if you rounded off your hours to the client's advantage or to yours. I've always rounded them down, feeling that any benefit should accrue to the client. Integrity in details contributes to success as a practitioner. When I am in doubt about the value of a service to the client, I discount

**41**

the service; one of my values is that the service must be cost-effective to be useful to the client. Although I won't accept an assignment that will not bring in adequate revenues, I don't want to gouge the client either. Trust your intuition; you are your own best judge. Mickey Rosenau, a fellow consultant whom I respect greatly, used to say that all actions should be undertaken using the *New York Times* rule: If you do not want to see the banner headline displaying your actions in tomorrow morning's *New York Times*, then don't commit them!

To me, there are three components of a good assignment: adequate fees, knowing that we have made a difference in our presence and involvement in the client company, and a sense of pride and satisfaction in our work. I'm a product of an upbringing that stressed "the little engine that could" and doing the very best that I am capable of doing. As a result, I judge myself and my assignments on the basis of having put in all the effort I could to make it a success. You may find that there are additional or other components of your good assignment, such as intellectual gratification and good contacts for future networking and assignments.

## IF IT DOESN'T WORK OUT

The answer to every question is not yes, and the outcome of every assignment is not success. Sometimes paying attention to the administrative and financial details proves to be burdensome for the neophyte consultant. Or you might be turned off by the lack of authority to accompany the responsibility you've assumed in taking on the assignment for your client. Or you might miss the support staff or team around which to focus your activities. The list is endless.

If you complete this first assignment and are not enthralled with the myriad aspects of conducting your own consulting practice, then perhaps you ought to look again at the job opportunities within a larger organization—as a consultant, a staff person, a line manager, or an executive wherein you are empowered to make things happen rather than merely to recommend. Unless you enjoy what you did enough to generate the requisite enthusiasm, you'll find it nearly impossible to sustain the energy and enthusiasm over the long haul of difficult clients, terrible economic conditions, and competitive forces.

## SUMMARY

You've gone through the effort required to get your first assignment and to execute it for your client. You prepared for that first assignment with the minimum investment of expense and time. Hopefully the experience has been a satisfactory one for all of you, client and new consultant, and you're ready to buckle down and establish yourself as a permanent business. If not, you've learned that entrepreneurial consulting isn't for you and you can address other opportunities that might prove more rewarding.

Now you're ready to solidify your practice into a business that requires the management and professional skills discussed in the following chapters to become a continuing success.

## PART TWO

# The Business of Management Consulting

## Is This Really How You Want to Spend Tomorrow?

# CHAPTER 3

---

# Organizing
# and Managing
# Your Business

**P**resumably you've completed your first assignment, and now are ready to make the decision as to whether you really want to consult as a full-time profession. Often first assignments are a result of beginner's luck or an intense but temporary need for a specialty that fades as the arcane subject becomes mainstream business practice. (Think about quality concepts, information systems, and corporate communications—all of them specialties at one or more points during the past decade.) You have two alternatives: wait for the serendipitous client windfall to come your way, or organize yourself and your resources as a business to respond to client demand, as well as to create more of that demand.

Now, if you *don't* want to run a business, don't read any further. Instead of putting your time and energy into the myriad nonconsulting-related tasks you must perform, put this book down, and spend your time preparing a résumé to use while you seek employment elsewhere. See the Bibliography for a comprehensive list of books with instructions that can better help, such as Asher's *Overnight Résumé*.

The successful consultants I've known over the long haul have viewed what they are doing with foresight and professionalism. That is not to say that they didn't take advantage of the many opportunities that came their way. However, they did not try to be all things to all people. They had a vision that remained consistent over time, and built up their reputation rather than placing them in the position of having to develop a new reputation or prove their capabilities each time.

But all the foresight in the world is not enough. Even if your practice comprises only yourself, you must also organize yourself to accommodate all of the functions that a viable business must perform:

- Financial management.
- Human resources.
- Administration and office management.
- Legal counsel.
- Marketing and sales.
- Public relations.
- Planning.

Not all of these functions need be performed by yourself or your employees, but someone must be identified as responsible for the tasks that keep enterprises, large and small, moving ahead in a profitable manner. Nevertheless, remember that *your primary focus is to consult*; every moment you spend on overhead items (tasks you cannot bill to client) takes you away from consulting—and the revenues you generate. The challenge for an entrepreneurial consultant is to balance the cost of delegating the business tasks to others against the time it takes to do them yourself without losing perspective or focus.

## ORGANIZATION CHART-ITIS

You might feel that there's no need to define formally who will be doing what, either because there's only one *who* or you don't have the funds for lots of *whats*, but if you do not devote some time to thinking about the business needs of your practice, you might well end up without any business at all. The consultants I know who have been most vocal about their lackadaisical approach to practice nevertheless have spent much time on the business aspects. They just made this work seem effortless. I remember Bob Kahn, one of the foremost retail consultants over these past four decades, who delighted in never wearing a tie or having to market his services. Yet he published a newsletter of continuously good quality, maintained relationships with successive generations of his client base, devoted endless time to local charities, and spearheaded the role of ethics in consulting. The newsletter was profitable, and his clients could always count on his presence with little notice, which clearly reflected his behind-the-scenes orchestration of those components of his professional life to just make it seem effortless.

Your organization chart will have at least the boxes shown in Exhibit 3-1 under you, as president, principal, or partner. Before you fill your name in each of the boxes, let's examine what each task comprises, alternatives for performing those tasks, and the best organization for you.

## ESTABLISHING THE FORM OF YOUR CONSULTING BUSINESS

If you are just starting out and not sure about the longevity of your consulting practice, you'll probably begin as a sole practitioner or

**Exhibit 3-1**

FUNCTIONS TO BE PERFORMED

IN YOUR CONSULTING PRACTICE

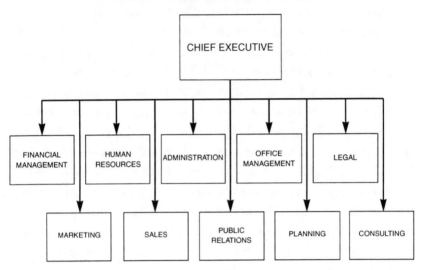

a sole proprietorship. You'll need a DBA (doing business as) or fictitious business name filing in a local paper. Because you should keep your personal and professional finances separate (which the tax bodies prefer), you should open a business checking account. Many banks still pay modest interest rates on checking accounts for sole proprietorship accounts (although not necessarily for partnerships and not at all for corporations).

Should you decide to incorporate, you'll need legal assistance to establish the corporation, its board of directors, voting rights, and other components. You'll also have to file separate tax returns for your corporation. Legal counsel can give you the best information on choosing the form of your business relative to your situation, but if you are involved in large contracts where litigation is the norm (in construction, for example), you jeopardize much more when you are a sole proprietorship than when you are a corporation. But in either case, you are responsible for legal fees to defend yourself, regardless of the outcome of the suit. Spurious suits are becoming commonplace. Anyone suspected of having deep pockets may be named in a suit, which can consume time, energy, and money for defense, even if the case ultimately is dismissed.

I have organized my business as a sole proprietorship, briefly as a partnership, and twice as a corporation over my quarter of a century of practice. Incorporation was largely for legal protection the second time; my reasons for initially incorporating, however, had more to do with pension plan advantages, fiscal year flexibility, and, yes, ego. I had always wanted to be president of something! I killed the corporation because it seemed an unnecessary expense when business waned during the early 1990s, only to resuscitate it when I became involved in large, multiconsultant jobs in the public sector.

A note of caution: If you do decide to incorporate, think carefully about the composition of your board of directors. Originally I had fancied a board consisting of outside experts who could provide me with awareness of the outside world while I was immersed in assignments, but the cost prohibited execution of my grand plan. Although I had asked my husband to be a director, legal counsel advised against doing so, indicating confusion of business and personal could be troublesome. When my husband became my ex-husband soon afterward, I was glad I had heeded counsel's advice. If you are the only one involved in your business, there's no need to complicate the decision process with an outside board. Should you need that vision into the world at large, you can always take an acquaintance with global eyes to lunch or dinner and learn one on one.

## WHAT'S IN A NAME?

I know consultants who use their own name (John Jones Consulting) and others who use a business name related to the function they provide (Ed Stone's business is the Dallas Marketing Group). I suspect it's a moot point as to which approach you should espouse. If *your* name is known in your target community, why give your business another name? Also, as your consulting practice matures, you may shift your focus (going from data processing into general management, for example, or shifting from a specialty focus to an industry focus), and you may not want to be saddled with a name that no longer serves you. Recently a colleague sent out the letter shown in Exhibit 3-2 describing a change in name because in twelve years of consulting, he had shifted focus.

If you decide to use a DBA or fictitious business name, your lawyer will need to do a search to ensure that the name is not already being used—regardless of the type of organization you choose (corporate, partnership, or sole practitioner). The likelihood of "Marsha D. Lewin Associates, Inc." being used elsewhere is far lower than something industry focused, such as "Automated Construction Management Consultants, Inc." But remember that you should file a DBA, regardless of the name you select, and it must appear in a newspaper of record (your local business journal can do so for a nominal fee). Exhibit 3-3 shows an example.

## MANAGING THE DOLLARS

Presumably you will be earning money, spending money in order to earn it, and continuing to pay taxes, and if you have employees, they will require payroll tax deposits in addition to your business taxes. Those categories translate into accounts receivable, accounts

**Exhibit 3-2**

SAMPLE ANNOUNCEMENT OF A NEW BUSINESS NAME

---

I have increasingly felt the name, The HR Link, no longer fits the business. My consulting is primarily to CEOs on issues of organization and leadership.

The HR Link suggests a human resources orientation, not my focus on leadership and organizational issues. Thus, I am changing my business name, as of 1-1-95, to the Jacobsen Consulting Group.

**Jacobsen** = The principal consultant.

**Consulting** = That's what we do.

**Group** = A select group of colleagues with complementary expertise in allied consulting businesses. Though we have separate businesses, we joint venture projects and refer to each other work outside our areas of expertise. They share my values and endorse the purpose, vision, and mission of my business. I trust them to provide services to my high standards.

*Source:* Ian Jacobsen. *The HR Link*, New Years, 1995. Sunnyvale, CA 94086-5404.

---

payable, and possibly payroll. While you may be a whiz at preparing your 1040 each year, you might well consider the cost of a reliable accountant with a good knowledge of tax consequences and alternatives as an investment rather than an expense.

A common error I've observed in fellow consultants is their failure to set aside the proper percentage required for the quarterly tax estimates, only to have to borrow monies they had thought were their revenues to spend. I've located a trusted accountant, Mort Algaze, whose advice I rely on for decisions with potential financial impact. I

**Exhibit 3-3**
SAMPLE DBA ANNOUNCEMENT

# LEGAL

# NOTICES

FICTITIOUS BUSINESS NAME
STATEMENT
92106125

The following company is doing business as MARSHA D. LEWIN ASSOCIATES, 1580 Manning Ave., Suite 105, Los Angeles, CA 90024-5820. This business is being conducted by an individual, Marsha D. Lewin, 1580 Manning Ave., Suite 105, Los Angeles, CA 90024-5820. Business commenced January 1, 1992.

This statement was filed with the County Clerk of Los Angeles on February 14, 1992. Published February 24, March 3, 9, 16, 1992. Notice—this fictitious name statement expires on February 14, 1997. A new fictitious business name statement must be filed prior to February 14, 1997. The filing of this statement does not of itself authorize the use in this state of a fictitious business name in violation of the rights of another under federal, state, or common law (see section 14400 ET SEQ, business and professions code).

have had an in-house accounting system for a decade that allows me to pay checks and create my own financial reports (income and expense statements, and balance sheets). I give Mort monthly reports for analysis and tax preparations. I reduce the costs by shouldering some of the work since we do not have to pay his staff's bookkeeping costs, and I manage to get the best in financial advice.

Remember that you must pay both state and federal taxes, as well as certain city or county taxes. You'll also need a city business license; to keep it current requires annual taxes paid (a small matter if it establishes you as a valid business, especially when the Internal Revenue Service audits your expenses).

Should you get a resale number, a state-assigned number allowing you to purchase items for subsequent resale and defer the payment of the sales tax on the item until you actually sell it? We have one but rarely use it for clients. Unless you are, for example, buying computer components and reassembling them for sale to clients, or have books or tapes that you sell to clients, I suspect that you'd be better off waiting to acquire a resale number from your state Board of Equalization, or the entity that covers this function in your state, and save yourself that administrative hassle of filing forms.

Even with an automated system, accounts-payable activities result in two half-days of work monthly. Accounts-receivable activities are minimal, since our clients generally pay promptly according to our written agreements. One exception was a client referred to me by another consultant who was still actively engaged in a turnaround task with this client. The client resented my associate's having been forced on him by the lending institution; he was determined not to pay easily or readily. It took many hours of telephone calls until the checks finally appeared, but they appeared, and the client paid in full. Had this occurred when I was working eighty hours a week with other clients, I might not have possessed the patience needed to facilitate the payment.

If you are a sole practitioner, your business finances are closely related to your personal finances, and their mutual impact is considerable. For that reason, I have emphasized the necessity of having a tight relationship with your accountant as you make your decisions, lest you end up on December 31 dreading Uncle Sam's impact on you. Since each situation is different, I do not give any further advice on this topic other than to direct you to a competent and trustworthy certified public accountant. A good source for a referral is a fellow entrepreneur or consultant. That's how I found Mort; he's familiar with the special needs of entrepreneurial consultants and treats me with discretion and confidentiality. He has always been available to me, and to the other consultants from whom I learned of him. But he is as closemouthed about others' matters as I know he is about mine.

Finally, no matter how small your business might be, a good banking relationship is vital. After many years of perceived anonymity at local branch offices, I was introduced to the head office of a local commercial bank, where I have had my business accounts for many years. I have saved countless hours of waiting for inexperienced tellers while getting the best advice this bank can offer me. Should I need financing (I have not, thus far), I have the benefit of the bank's experience with me as a distinct asset. In addition, when I drop by to visit the vice president in charge, he fills me in on local economic trends and validates my parking—added interest on my investments with the bank! Clearly using an ATM would not benefit me nearly as much.

## MANAGEMENT CONTROLS

Even if you are a solo, monitoring how well you are performing against your estimates is as important as in a large firm. You should be able to figure out, whether using your pencil and paper or your slick new computer system, the following information, which will be critical to you as you determine how profitable you are at the moment and just how profitable you might be in the very near future:

- Actual fees vs. estimated.
- Actual direct costs vs. estimated.
- Costs to prepare proposals.
- Labor hours and dollar backlog.
- Billed hours by project and by person (if you have subcontractors or team with someone else).
- Productivity by person and by project.
- Proposals outstanding.
- Proposal success ratio (number achieved/number written).
- Aged receivables (by thirty, sixty, ninety, and over ninety days).
- Comparison with previous years.

## MAINTAINING YOUR PAPER TRAIL

You'll make the Internal Revenue Service much happier and more easily satisfied by keeping good records of your expenses. Although there are sophisticated techniques available, I still record my expenses in my paper daybook and keep the original receipts. I note on each receipt as well as in the daybook with whom I met or dined and the topics covered. The daybook is my line of first reference; the receipts, filed by month, are available for authentication, if needed for audit.

I do know many consultants who swear by their hand-held organizers, but I also know of these organizers that have failed their masters, with the resultant total loss of the entire year's detail. If you *must* have such a device, be sure to get one that has an interface capability, allowing you periodically to download the data your organizer contains to your main computer. Should you lose the battery or, worse, the organizer itself, you can upload the database from your main computer and start again, with a minimum of disaster.

## SEPARATION OF BUSINESS (FROM PLEASURE?)

Although it might appear to save dollars, co-mingling business and personal expenses can be a truly false economy. Not only does your image suffer when potential clients hear your four-year-old daughter blithely answering your telephone, but you'll probably end up spending more time and money each month to separate out your business from personal phone calls than a separate line would cost. And in some areas, you can't have a personal telephone number if you want to be listed in the Yellow Pages.

You should also have separate personal and business checking accounts. Business expenses should be paid out of your business account, and personal expenses from your personal account. Although I have many credit cards, I use a single one for both personal and business purchases because of the airplane mileage I earn. Each month I calculate which portion of my bill was personal and which business, and pay each with a separate check. This calculating takes extra time, but I've been able to use the earned miles for both business trips and vacations over the years—a good reward for the reconciling time.

## WORKING WHERE YOU LIVE

I've always maintained an office in my home (although only rarely do clients meet me there). The commute to work is brief and the dress code quite informal. I do not have young children underfoot, and my work area has always been an area separate from the rest of the house. One thing to consider about an in-home office is preserving the integrity of both your nontraditional work environment and your private life by articulating to your secretarial or other office help which places are off limits to them.

Something else to think about is the tax deduction for your in-home office. I have taken photographs of my work area in case I ever have to prove that my work space is 100 percent deductible as a home office. It's probably a good idea to accumulate as much visible proof of your exclusive separation of residence and work usage in case you ever need to show it to the IRS.

Your accountant or tax adviser can best tell you what to do in your particular situation, but as a rule, if you deduct your office—say 25 percent of your mortgage payment each month—you ultimately pay your taxes when you sell your home, since you've been enjoying the tax deduction as you go along. If you rent, then you can pay the 25 percent as you go along from your business as a business expense.

Periodically I consider moving into a "real" office and frequently have been offered space with others in more formal environments. However, I often travel to client sites and find that having one more place to visit at the end of the day is tiresome. And from a personal safety perspective, going into office buildings in off-hours is a continuing deterrent to moving into a formal office. Of course, if your clientele can best be accommodated by your proximity to them, then you may decide differently. But remember that you need to earn enough to cover the rent, utilities (including cleaning service, electricity, water and gas perhaps), and possibly costly parking in your building for yourself and potential clients—not to mention costs for staff you might find you need.

Does it hurt you not to have a "real" office? That is a personal decision. If you like the daily contact with others in an elevator, if you can't truly obtain the needed separate space in your own home, if your client base *must* meet you in an office building, then the advantages of home offices are not for you.

## HIRING AND HUMAN RESOURCES

Human resources (HR) refers to the policies and issues that deal with relationships among people: your employees as well as your clients and their employees. You might think that there are no HR tasks in a small consultancy, but consider this issue carefully. Independent contractors to whom you subcontract work might constitute an HR issue within that arena. For example, have you heard of Section 1706 of the Tax Reform Act of 1986? It is a set of federal criteria for determining whether a contractor is truly independent or is an employee. Can you clearly show that people you've hired on a subcontractor basis are most definitely not employees whom you've chosen to hire in this manner to avoid payroll taxes?

If you decide to have employees, you will have many legal requirements to fulfill. For example, if you pay for your own medical and other insurances, you'll have to do the same for your employees. Can you afford that expense as you're getting started? I've known consultants who determined they simply *had to have* secretarial help on an employee basis but couldn't afford to keep these people on once the initial contract was over. Firing a valued employee is very difficult; being able to sustain a valued contributor as a subcontractor by renewing his or her contract because business is prospering is far easier.

Here are some of the HR issues that you should consider when deciding whether to hire someone or subcontract to them:

- Education and training.
- Safety and ergonomics.
- Counseling.
- Equal employment opportunity.
- Hiring and firing, promotions and demotions.
- Performance standards and job descriptions.
- Job rules and grievance handling.
- Workers' compensation and other insurances.
- Benefits (travel, perks, days off).
- Personnel record keeping, background checks.

You are probably better off to identify resources available by the hour or on a per job basis, and hire independent contractors as needed. For example, if you need word processing done, you'll find plenty of people in this business, easily run out of one's home. These contractors will pick up and drop off your reports for you. In fact, with all of the electronics available today, I ask all of our subcontractors to be online with CompuServe, through which we can send electronic mail and exchange files, eliminating the cost of messengers and other delivery.

Your expectations and those with whom you come in contact need to be brought into harmony on the most basic level: how you want to be dealt with and how others can expect to be treated by you.

## ADMINISTRATION: OFFICE EQUIPMENT AND SYSTEMS

Consultants have to administer many relationships—their practices, their clients, their governmental status—and it all takes time, effort, and usually paperwork. Typically, consultants should spend as little time as possible in administering their practices so that they can be out selling and providing their services to their client base.

A synonym for administration is management—of your own practice, in this case. You must keep records of your actions because you are a business: for taxes, for clients, for your own reference, and—unfortunately—for possible legal issues that might arise. How will you organize your filing system? What about your mailing list? With the goal of minimizing time spent in office administration, an efficient and effective office environment should contain at a minimum the following equipment and systems.

## Getting Your Messages

Get an answering machine that is remotely accessible. If you can ensure you'll be able to do so, you can also include a message indicating the maximum amount of time the caller will have to wait for a call to be returned when you are not there to answer it. A separate telephone line is recommended if your office is in your home so that the callers won't have to deal with your children answering or tying up the family line.

Balance the warmth of the greeting with the professionalism you are trying to maintain. A typical message might be as follows:

> You've reached the offices of Newly Formed Consultants. We're out of the office at the moment [or, to be more high tech, "we are on the other line"]. Please leave your name and number with our voice mail, and we shall return your call within ninety minutes. Thank you for calling.

An alternative to an answering machine is your local telephone company's voice mail package. You won't need an answering machine in this case and can still access your mail messages from anywhere. You can usually forward your calls to a specific location with such services, so you can reply to calls immediately. The drawback here is that clients do not generally like their consultants to conduct other work while on-site. You might give the impression that you are charging them for someone else's assignment even if you deduct the time spent from their fees.

You might also consider getting a pager to keep in touch with clients. Once upon a time, only physicians had pagers. When the beep was heard, heads turned, and anyone using the pay telephone relinquished it quickly to the dashing physician. Today lots of people have a pager, and since everyone with a pager needs quick access to a telephone, they also have cellular telephones at the ready. All of this equipment, including the laptop, makes briefcases very heavy—but that's another story.

Should you get a pager? I have worn one briefly, when we were supporting a remote customer and I was traveling extensively. The customer seldom used it, and when it was used, I found I had difficulty finding an accessible telephone on the freeway. With answering machines available, I can periodically call into my office and retrieve messages. When an emergency develops, I am usually right on top of the situation without a beeper.

I now have a car phone but not a portable phone. The car phone also serves safety needs, enabling me to communicate if I find myself in danger while driving along some of Los Angeles' meaner freeways and streets. As a general rule, however, I prefer to use my driving time to think rather than to speak. I find it hard to drive adequately and manage dialing telephone numbers. (I can still walk and chew gum, though.)

## Organizing Your Files

Get a filing system that makes sense. I use colored file folders and have different colors for different general topics: my company, personal, clients (multiple colors so that I can identify client folders quickly when multiple clients are being handled). Color coding helps deter me from picking up the wrong file folders when running out to the client.

During an assignment, I usually amass most of the following documents:

- Proposal (statement of work).
- Task schedules.
- Organizational data.
- Correspondence.
- Minutes of meetings and telephone conversations.
- Working papers.
- Status reports.
- Reference materials.
- Signed client authorizations and contracts.
- Final reports.
- Invoices.
- Cost data.

Exhibit 3-4 is a simple form I use for logging business calls for each project. Exhibit 3-5 is a time sheet I use to record my hours worked on each client assignment.

After a few assignments, all of this information (usually paper, with electronic backup) begins to mount up. How long should you keep papers from a client assignment? I make it a habit to leave my files from an assignment for six months after completion. Then I review the folders and discard the records I feel are duplicative or unnecessary, and sometimes I reorganize the following records which I maintain for a minimum of seven years after completion of the project:

- Contracts and invoices, and all supporting information such as bills or records of hours worked.

**Exhibit 3-4**

SAMPLE PHONE CALL LOG

Date_____

Marsha D. Lewin Associates, Inc.

Business Call Log

| Phone number | Person called | Bill to | Date called | Billed |
|---|---|---|---|---|
| | | | | |
| | | | | |
| | | | | |
| | | | | |
| | | | | |
| | | | | |
| | | | | |
| | | | | |
| | | | | |
| | | | | |
| | | | | |
| | | | | |
| | | | | |
| | | | | |
| | | | | |
| | | | | |
| | | | | |
| | | | | |
| | | | | |
| | | | | |
| | | | | |
| | | | | |
| | | | | |
| | | | | |
| | | | | |
| | | | | |
| | | | | |
| | | | | |
| | | | | |
| | | | | |
| | | | | |
| | | | | |

**Exhibit 3-5**

SAMPLE TIME SHEET

CLIENT: _____

CONSULTANT: _____

PERIOD COVERED: _____

| DATE/ HOURS | TASKS | TOTAL HOURS | CHARGE TO | LOCATION | MILEAGE | OTHER EXPENSE | TOTAL $ |
|---|---|---|---|---|---|---|---|
| | | | | | | | |
| | | | | | | | |
| | | | | | | | |
| | | | | | | | |
| | | | | | | | |
| | | | | | | | |
| | | | | | | | |
| | | | | | | | |
| | | | | | | | |
| | | | | | | | |
| | | | | | | | |
| | | | | | | | |
| | | | | | | | |
| | | | | | | | |
| | | | | | | | |

- Status reports and memos.
- Reports and studies.

As I review the files, I use the following criteria for determining which records to save:

- Will this document be of value as reference for a future assignment?
- Does this document reflect decisions that might be critical if an action is questioned in the future?
- Is this required for proof of financial activities?

Certain files contain sensitive information, which you may not wish to share with others—for example, employee evaluations, personal notes of a confidential nature, or financial matters such as assignment profitability. Should you take these folders with you to a client site (I never do), be sure to restrict them from others' view. I have one confidential folder for each client *marked with a red line* so I know which it is. It contains billing information and other project-specific administrative data that I need when on-site but don't want to share.

## Maintaining Your Database

Mailing lists must be kept current to be valuable to you. Who will do this work? You can use one of the many computer programs available for this task, but only you know who should be added or deleted based on your marketing goals (which can change over time).

## Equipment Selection and Maintenance

You need some essential components to give you a professional image: a copier, a computer, and possibly a fax machine, in addition to your telephone, to get started.

I have a fax machine in addition to a fax card in my computer because receiving faxes when my computer is off remains a technical problem to be solved. It is *not* recommended that you leave your computer on at all times. As fax machines continue to decrease in cost, the convenience is well worth the additional piece of equipment.

I have a good office-quality copier so I can make small numbers of copies in-house. For very large tasks, I use a commercial copy store.

I can't imagine any new consultant embarking on this profession without the latest in computer technology. My computer leverages my ability to communicate, analyze, and manage. The type fonts I use and the forms I generate contribute to my professional image as much as the clothing I wear and the way I talk. My technical productivity tools convey an image of efficient resource usage: I don't waste my time or my client's time and money. Standard office automation now includes the ability to generate smart-looking transparencies for presentations to clients as well as colorful on-screen presentations to display to prospective clients on a laptop (which piece of equipment is now a vital member of my own proposal team).

More information on specific computer equipment you'll need can be found in Chapter 8. Remember that computer technology changes almost overnight now, and today's best products may be tomorrow's Edsels, so be sure you're well advised.

## LEGAL ISSUES

Be sure to use competent legal counsel for reviewing your contracts and agreements with your clients (and subcontractors, if you have them). A shake of the hand used to be adequate, but is no longer; we live in a litigious society in a litigious age. We do not want our clients to sue us or us to sue them. But today's pet project can become tomorrow's lawsuit. With *downsizing* and *rightsizing* common buzzwords in companies, there is a bigger chance that your client contact at a company might not be there tomorrow. Despite all the good feelings that exist between you and your client at the moment, don't assume that you need not document directions and information you receive from him or her. More than once I've had this happen, and having obtained—and saved—a record of what was said or recommended has been valuable for me and my reputation—and my client's company as well.

Even more so, be careful if and when you subcontract with others. For example, who has the rights to products you might develop together (training materials, software, and interview instruments are products)? What will you do if a subcontractor sells himself or herself directly to a client you've had? The subcontractor letters of agreement I use contain clauses regarding these issues. Exhibit 3-6 is a sample subcontractor letter of agreement; Exhibit 3-7 is a sample confidentiality agreement. Exhibit 3-8 is a technical nondisclosure agreement, and Exhibit 3-9 is a noncompete agreement. Always review any form you select with your own counsel. An ounce of legal prevention is worth the thousands of dollars a lawsuit can cost. Whether you win the suit or not, you always lose in time and legal fees.

If you decide to incorporate, you should seek assistance from your lawyer. Like the architect Le Corbusier, I believe that form follows function. The corporate umbrella, if set up properly, can protect your personal assets from vulnerability if you are sued professionally. However, competent legal counsel can advise you on what's best for your situation. Incorporation is costly, and you can end up being double taxed on your income (as both personal income and corporate profits) if you are not careful. You also have separate tax forms to file, and some deductions apply to sole proprietorships, or to corporations, but not to both. It's a confusing maze, and one you probably don't want to embark upon unless you must. You pay to establish the corporation, to maintain it, and, of course, to "kill" it.

## Exhibit 3-6

SAMPLE SUBCONTRACTOR LETTER OF AGREEMENT

**Purpose**

This is to confirm tasks, fees, and other arrangements between the parties stated below in execution of the assignment cited.

**Parties**

Marsha D. Lewin Associates, Inc.

[Subcontractor name]

**Scope**

To assist Marsha D. Lewin Associates, Inc. (MDLA) with Document Management services and any such other tasks as may be assigned for the System Design and Implementation for the Project Information System for [client's name].

**Terms**

MDLA is the prime contractor on this assignment. Status reports should be submitted weekly to MDLA on Friday. All invoices should be submitted to MDLA two days before the 15th and the last day of the month. Invoices will then be computed and mailed to the client within 5 business days. Subcontractor will be paid by MDLA within 10 days after receipt of payment from the client.

Software developed is property of [client's name]. See [identify number of client/consultant] contract for any other restrictive, pass-through clauses.

All fees, tasks performed to support those fees, and expenses should be itemized. A separate subtotal for each category of expenses should be included (number of miles, subsistence, copying, telephone, other),

**Exhibit 3-6**

CONTINUED

and copies of all expense receipts (e.g., telephone bills, hotel bills), must be included in duplicate.

This agreement is nonexclusive insofar as subcontractor is free to work elsewhere for other clients, with disclosure to MDLA of any potential conflicts of interest. Subcontractor is not entitled to MDLA benefits under the terms of this agreement.

**Fees**

[Subcontractor name] will be paid as agreed to for each work order attached to this Letter of Agreement, as paid by [client's name]. Travel time will be not be reimbursed; mileage will be reimbursed at 30 cents per mile. All expenses not covered by the client must be approved by MDLA in advance.

by:

Marsha D. Lewin Associates, Inc.

Marsha D. Lewin                    [Subcontractor name]

_____          _____

Signature                         Signature


_____          _____

Date                              Social Security Number

## Exhibit 3-7
### SAMPLE CONFIDENTIALITY AGREEMENT

---

1. Company [the consultant] agrees to furnish Recipient [the subcontractor] with certain information and documents (hereinafter collectively called "Information") relating to [subject of consultant's assignment] and hereby grants Recipient the right to use Information for a period of 90 days, after receipt thereof, solely for evaluation purposes and the purposes so stated.

2. Recipient shall maintain the Information in confidence and avoid disclosing the Information to others outside of Company and shall not use the Information, except for the sole purpose stated above. Such restriction on disclosure and use shall not apply to any information:

i. That is independently developed by Recipient or lawfully received free of restriction from another source having the right to so furnish the Information,

ii. After it has become generally available to the public without breach of this Agreement by Recipient, or

iii. That at the time of disclosure to Recipient was known to Recipient.

3. All information shall remain the property of Company upon expiration of the period specified above.

Recipient shall return all Information received and all copies thereof to the Company.

4. This Agreement should be governed under the Laws of the State of California.

**Exhibit 3-7**
CONTINUED

5. Access to the information contained in this package is expressed acceptance of the terms and conditions of this disclosure agreement.

6. Should the Recipient not agree to the terms and conditions so stipulated, the Recipient is requested to return the package to [the consultant].

Date _____

Signed _____

Position _____

_____

## Exhibit 3-8
### SAMPLE TECHNICAL NONDISCLOSURE AGREEMENT

By the signatures of their authorized representatives below, [subcontractor] and Marsha D. Lewin Associates, Inc. (MDLA) do enter into the following agreement:

On their own behalf and/or their customers' behalf, MDLA has designed and developed computer software technology (referred to as "Proprietary Technology") which MDLA has agreed to, and wishes to, keep proprietary and confidential.

[Subcontractor] is receiving knowledge of this Proprietary Technology in order to modify, add to, or create new technology on behalf of MDLA and its customers.

[Subcontractor] and MDLA mutually agree as follows:

1. All information disclosed to [subcontractor] concerning the Proprietary Technology that MDLA develops, for itself or on behalf of its customers, is considered confidential and proprietary to MDLA. All technology that [subcontractor] develops on behalf of MDLA or its customers is considered confidential and proprietary and becomes a part of the Proprietary Technology. This Proprietary Technology shall remain confidential and [subcontractor] shall not disclose this information until such time as MDLA makes the information generally available to the public as described in item 3 below.

2. [Subcontractor] will return all Proprietary Information to MDLA and/or its customers upon termination of the parties' relationship.

3. This agreement specifically excludes technical information which: (i) is now or which subsequently becomes otherwise known in the industry; (ii) is known by [subcontractor] prior to the time that [subcontractor] received information regarding the Proprietary Technol-

74

**Exhibit 3-8**

CONTINUED

ogy; (iii) is furnished by MDLA to third parties without restriction on disclosure; (iv) is subsequently rightfully furnished to [subcontractor] by a third party without a restriction on disclosure, or (v) is independently developed by [subcontractor], provided that the person(s) developing same have not had access to the Proprietary Technology.

4. [Subcontractor] shall be relieved of all obligations under this agreement with regards to confidentiality eight years subsequent to completing the last work for or on behalf of MDLA, or upon written authorization by MDLA specifically authorizing such release from nondisclosure obligations.

Understood and agreed:

[Subcontractor]                     Marsha D. Lewin Associates, Inc.

By: _____        By: _____

Title: _____       Title: _____

Date: _____        Date: _____

## Exhibit 3-9
### SAMPLE NONCOMPETE AGREEMENT

---

By the signatures of their authorized representatives below, [subcontractor] and Marsha D. Lewin Associates, Inc. (MDLA) do enter into the following agreement:

MDLA provides consulting and contractual services to "Customers".

MDLA solicits business from Customers to perform services. MDLA wishes to have [subcontractor] perform said work on MDLA's behalf. "Consultant Customers" are Customers or potential customers where MDLA has solicited work and submitted [subcontractor] name and/or resume.

[Subcontractor] is qualified to provide services to Customers. [Subcontractor] agrees to provide services on behalf of MDLA as a representative of MDLA to Consultant Customers.

[Subcontractor] agrees not to attempt to obtain work from or perform services for any Consultant Customers (on [subcontractor's] own behalf, as an employee of Consultant Customer, as an individual contractor to Consultant Customer, or as a representative, employee or subcontractor to another firm who performs services for the Consultant Customer) except as a representative of MDLA, or with explicit written consent of MDLA.

[Subcontractor] further agrees not to use MDLA's customer lists (or other MDLA documentation to develop customer lists) to attempt to obtain work from or perform services for any Consultant Customers (on Consultant's own behalf, as an employee of Consultant Customer, as an individual contractor to Consultant Customer, or as a representative, employee or subcontractor to another firm who performs services for the Consultant Customer) except as a representative of MDLA.

**Exhibit 3-9**

CONTINUED

This agreement will remain in force for a period of twelve months after the last date that [subcontractor] provides services on behalf of MDLA, or for a period of twelve months after [subcontractor's] name/and or résumé is submitted to a prospective Consultant Customer, whichever is later. This agreement will automatically renew should [subcontractor] provide further services on MDLA's behalf.

Understood and agreed:

[Subcontractor]                    Marsha D. Lewin Associates, Inc.

By: _____        By: _____

Title: _____        Title: _____

Date: _____        Date: _____

At a minimum you should have a trusted lawyer who can:

- Review your client agreements.
- Review your subcontractor agreements.
- Help with incorporation or partnership.
- Review any patents or other nondisclosure agreements.

## THE REASSURANCE OF INSURANCE

What will happen if you can't work for a while? If you suddenly die? If you suffer a debilitating illness? If you are sued by a former client? Having various types of insurance cannot protect you from these eventualities, but they can mitigate the impact somewhat. There are five types of insurance that consultants should carry, although not all of them can be underwritten these days. These are in addition, of course, to automobile and homeowners (or renters) policies, and, if you live where I do, earthquake insurance policies. Clients may have additional insurance coverage requirements, so be sure to read the fine print in their contracts. Often you can ask them to delete Workers' Compensation Insurance if you have no employees, and they will, saving you unnecessary expense (such insurance does not cover the employer).

## Health Insurance

Many health insurance options exist, depending on where you live, among them HMOs (health maintenance organizations), insurance policies with high deductibles (say $1,000 or $2,000), and preferred provider plans (you select from a set of physicians with whom the insurer has existing agreements to provide you care when needed). Sometimes you can get major medical coverage at significantly lower cost that kicks in only if you incur extraordinary costs or hospital stays. Such policies are available through professional organizations or, if you're over fifty, from the American Association of Retired Persons.

Health insurance policies and carriers are far from alike. After paying premiums for several years without claims, I had surgery and was astounded when my annual fees soared as a result. The pool in which I had been placed as a small business owner allowed the insurer to increase my rates. After great difficulty, I finally affiliated with Blue Cross of California's Prudent Buyer Plan, with a pool that is substantially larger and more varied in composition. The moral of this story is to shop around and choose your plan thoughtfully.

Certainly the high cost of health care and the resultant high cost of health insurance are significant issues for small and large consulting firms. But you need to accommodate the significant bite such coverage is going to take out of your budget, if not for yourself, then certainly for your family.

## Life Insurance

This is the cheapest and most common form of insurance to obtain, and you probably will have no problem in having a policy written. Even if you have no young family to protect, you can get various forms that will cover your remaining mortgage payment, burial expenses, and any outstanding debts—all of which might create problems for your loved ones after your demise. If you do have children in college or younger, life insurance is a must to ensure their future security.

## Disability Insurance

The effects of disability can be devastating. Certainly through your primary earning years, say to age sixty or sixty-two, you should have enough insurance to cover your costs of living, supporting any recurring debts you have (e.g., utilities, mortgage, car payments).

Since the length of the waiting period from the onset of disability until payments to you start affects the annual premium, you can reduce the costs somewhat by electing a longer waiting period. In that case, you must have enough money reserved in savings to cover your expenses during the waiting period.

## Professional Liability Insurance

What can you do if a client sues you, alleging damages to his or her business based on errors or omissions in your work? Some say no one can operate without insurance; others observe that if a client knows your insurance company's hands are reinforcing your deep pockets, you're more likely to be named in a lawsuit. Regardless of approach, the sad fact is that if you are sued, you'll still have to pay legal fees, because most of these policies—if you can get them— have a deductible amount that's usually not trivial (e.g., $10,000). The major problem with professional liability insurance for consultants is that there are so many waivers that your work may not be covered. For example, work by subcontractors may be excluded; or part of the work you are normally required to perform, such as a product recommendation, may be likewise excluded. Some policies are available through professional associations in your state. For example, the Institute of Management Consultants has a liability policy available through its carrier, but the company underwriting the policy is not licensed in the state of California. Should this company go out of business for any reason—mismanagement, for example, or extraordinarily high claims against it—a Californian with a policy from this carrier would have no recourse after paying in hefty fees.

## Office Equipment Insurance

Sometimes your computers and other office equipment may require a separate policy underwritten by a company other than your regular carrier, especially if you have offices in your home. Simply assuming that your office equipment is covered can be a costly error, so check with your specific carrier or agent to ensure adequate coverage.

## Choosing an Insurance Agent

Insurance is a costly but necessary evil. As in any other issue related to your business, you should seek professional expertise, not merely salesmanship, to decide what to do. You'll probably get many circulars in the mail peddling insurance policies, especially once you get your business license and your name gets on mailing lists targeted to new businesses such as yours. For any insurance, it's always best to deal with someone you know, who will be available when and if needed. For example, during the recent Northridge earthquake, I was enormously relieved by the proximity and attention of my insurance agent. Trying to communicate over long-distance lines would have been impossible while those telephone connections were down for long periods of time in either direction.

Relative to clients' suits, the best defensive policy is to do good work and maintain excellent relationships with your clients. Certainly the cost of working out any possible problems beforehand is far less than the costs of litigation and the heavy emotional toll such litigation can take.

## PLANNING

Frankly, I have never been able to do a very good job of planning. After a quarter of a century in consulting, I've come to the conclusion that the best I can do is respond adequately to the opportunities that present themselves, for there are far too many variables over which I have no control. In fact, when I sit down before year end with Mort, my trusted accountant, to project the revenues for the coming year as part of our tax planning exercise, I am generally baffled as to what to expect.

I remember being told that nothing much happens over the holiday season. If you don't have anything lined up by November 15, don't expect the world to start waking up and calling until January 15. Yet I've gotten many assignments during December, and recently three opportunities appeared between Christmas and New Year's Day.

Typically we have some measure of control over expenses, but our income is determined by the condition of the economy in general and our market niche in particular. The best you can do is ensure that you have a plan for marketing your services and controlling costs and that you have a set of backup plans to cover the possibilities of having too much work at one time or not enough work.

Consulting does not allow for planning in the truest sense. Rather, our "planning" is really taking advantage of the opportunities that do present themselves, usually in a somewhat random manner. To the extent that we can plan to be *able* to take advantage of those opportunities when they do arise, then consultants may be considered to do some planning.


## SUMMARY

There is no substitute for doing a good job for your clients. That's the essence of consulting. The art of consulting is knowing what is "a good job" for any single client and single client situation.

In this chapter, we've examined the critical issues of organizing your practice and the major tasks you're going to have to attend to as an entrepreneurial consultant. Refer to Exhibit 12-1 for a checklist to help you cover all the bases.

# CHAPTER 4

---

# How to Set Fees

Now that you've established what you are, how much should you charge? Setting fees for your services is always difficult. Your rates as an employee included many benefits that you must now pay for out of the fees you're going to charge. In addition, your fee structure should accommodate the time for marketing and that lull in between assignments. Try to be as realistic as possible in guessing, for that's all it can be, how many clients you'll have. The formula itself is easy; it's the accuracy that's hard to predict. Calculate as follows:

1.  Total number of paid hours you'll work over the next year (allow for vacation time, attendance at educational seminars, commuting time, nonbillable hours).
2.  How much money you estimate you'll need for the year (excluding expenses you can bill directly to the client).
3.  Divide (1) into (2), and you've got your hourly rate to charge.

Let's say, by way of example, that I work 8 hours daily, 3 days weekly, for 40 weeks. The number yielded in Step 1 is 960 hours. If I estimate in Step 2 that $100,000 is needed annually to cover my overhead, marketing and sales time, children's college tuition, vacation to the Alps, taxes, and mortgage, my hourly rate, from Step 3, is $104.17.

The calculation, however, is the easy part. Making the formula work is the consultant's challenge. What do I do if my competition is charging only $50 hourly? Or, better, $200 hourly? Early on in my career I was advised by a seasoned professional that the advice of consultants is heeded according to how much they are paid: A $100 per hour consultant is listened to more frequently than a $25 per hour consultant. He was right. When I charge less, my recommendations do not seem to be adopted as frequently. And being an expensive consultant gives some cachet to the client. On the other hand, your fees add up rather quickly, so you're more likely to be let go earlier if the problem you were hired to solve appears to have been fixed.

Another problem with the purely mathematical fee calculation is that you have no control over the demand for your services, and thus evolves the roller coaster on which many consultants find themselves: If you haven't made "your numbers" when you have an opportunity to earn moneys, all thoughts of rest time and other pleasures go out the window. Vacations are canceled, theater tickets are given away to understanding and appreciative friends—and the balance that we all need to be effective over the long haul often is lost. Consulting clearly is cyclical. Since we do not know when the next assignment will present itself, try as we might to make it happen, we must make the most of each opportunity.

So if I must earn $100,000 annually but don't have the business, what can I do? That's where keeping busy is important: using the downtime to increase your network, redo your marketing brochure or your public relations kit, take a class at a local school, or, even better, teach or write an article or a book. Or if the market for your services has fallen away entirely, take a vacation. In fact, I've found that when I am gloomily waiting for the phone to ring, I am best off leaving the office and getting away for a short while. The time off eases my anxiety level and puts into perspective why I am working in the first place.

But back to fee setting. Look at your competition's fee schedules—often you can merely call the competition to find out what their current rates are—and compare your fees to theirs. If you charge too little, you might discredit yourself unintentionally. Too much, and you might price yourself out of the assignment. If someone from a larger firm is charging less than you, how do you justify your higher rates, especially if you don't have the overhead costs to justify your fees or the experience behind you?

This brings us to *differentiating* your services from someone else's. All consultants are not alike. Your experience, your approach, the benefit you've brought previous clients, your knowledge of their particular industry: all of these can make you different from a competitor. Perhaps you can show you not only design and install computer systems for your client's company but you reorganize, or help obtain financing, or do strategic planning—multiple functions rather than a single one. This means the client deals with one consultant rather than having to reeducate another one.

## IF THIS IS TUESDAY, WHAT AM I CHARGING?

Should you charge all clients the same rate or vary fee by client or assignment? A variable-fee rate can get confusing, especially to you when billing, but it does serve you in the following cases:

**85**

- You are performing different tasks with different worth for each client—for example, designing a system, a more costly task, as opposed to merely validating a vendor's proposal.
- Company size or financial viability prevents you from obtaining normal rates—for example, a company that is cutting back asks you to help in this task but does not have much money to spend on its own people, let alone for you.

Be wary, though, of varying your fees within the same marketplace or geographic area. If two of your clients get together and start talking about how much you're costing them, you might find out that you lose a good client or get pressure from one to reduce your fees.

I have reduced my fees for relatively short-term or small projects, to take advantage of performing an assignment that is of particular interest to me, or to help out an old client in reduced circumstances. However, I am careful to ensure that not all of my time is tied up at reduced rates, and certainly not for long. In this situation, I also have the client perform some of the work that I normally would have done (for example, writing up the meeting notes, producing a final report using his or her clerical staff). This is to show that the reduced rate reflects a reduced assignment, so that if I raise my fees on the next assignment, the client does not feel he or she is paying more for the same work product.

If you do vary your rates, I suggest you don't vary them by more than a third—for example, $100 hourly for a long-term contract and $150 hourly for a short-term contract. If you drop your rates too much, you are probably grossly underpricing or overpricing yourself on some assignments.

# RETAINER, HOURLY, TIME AND MATERIALS, OR WHAT?

The ideal assignment may be one that has longevity, so that you can iron out the inevitable wrinkles in a cyclical business. On the other hand, a long-term agreement can prevent you from taking advantage of opportunities at higher fees or in a desired location or business that would be more lucrative. A retainer can satisfy your need for reducing financial risk (but if that was a great need, would you be an entrepreneurial consultant in the first place?). Depending on your specialty and the manner in which you deliver services, you may charge according to one or more of the following bases.

## Fixed Price

This choice is particularly appropriate for seminars or in-house training classes, although you should charge expenses incurred separately, to eliminate problems that might be encountered, such as exorbitant plane fares, hotel rates, or reproduction. To the extent that you can reuse materials, your initial development costs are absorbed by the greater profit on subsequent seminars that require less work. It is very important in a fixed-price assignment to specify clearly the deliverables resulting from the assignment.

## Time and Materials (T&M)

This choice suits assignments when the time involved is highly variable or unpredictable. You can charge by the day or the hour. Generally the daily rate is eight times your hourly rate, no matter how many hours you may work on a given day. If you often work long days, then an hourly rate may be better for you, if the client agrees. The advantage to the client of an hourly rate is that he or

87

she pays only for the hours actually worked; the advantage to you is that you can balance multiple clients by "time slicing" on any given day, and you are paid for the hours you actually put in. You should specify a minimum number of hours on-site to avoid being called in for less time than the travel time necessary.

T&M agreements generally have a "not-to-exceed" figure for the assignment, after which additional funding must be negotiated. A good argument can be made for making the assignment a fixed-price one to start with, since you can't get more than the not-to-exceed figure, but if you finish early, you could make less. I found myself in a negotiation with a colleague and our client, and had just that occur. Although I typically avoid fixed-price work, I realized that we would be better off taking the fixed price since we were assuming the same risk at possibly lower return otherwise.

## Retainer

This is particularly useful when you know the client environment and can estimate well what level of support will be required to give value to your client over a period of time. You should always specify a number of hours or days so that your client knows what to expect realistically of your availability. I suggest keeping the commitment to semiannually or annually at best, to enable you to take advantage of other opportunities that might arise and to ensure that you do not lock yourself into the same rate for too long—and then have to negotiate a fee increase.

## Mixed Basis

A fixed fee plus T&M is useful if you want to split the assignment into phases. Often we do that to reduce the ambiguity in truly estimating an assignment, especially with a new client or new technology. We specify the evaluation phase on a fixed-price basis and subsequent design or implementation on either a T&M basis or fixed price, as appropriate. Or you can do T&M during the investigatory phase and then fixed price for implementation. Some consultants sell their seminars or training sessions on a fixed-price basis, with a variable T&M portion for preliminary research to customize to a client's particular needs.

## Contingency or Incentive Fee

The total amount you are paid depends on the success you achieve. This type of arrangement has been out of favor among consultants, since short-term gains could be made at the expense of the future viability of a company. However, clients that are involved in turn-around situations, for example, may not be able to pay when the contract is negotiated, so a contingency fee is appropriate. The key to this type of arrangement is to ensure that the client's best interests are being cared for and that the consultant stands to get paid for the work performed. If you are in doubt regarding the acceptability of such an arrangement, call your professional organization for an opinion.

## Equity Position

Alone or with some fees, you receive shares in the client company as payment. This choice is often used in start-up situations, where the consultant's contribution is critical yet financial backing is weakest. Thus, a consultant is paid in shares in the fledgling organization. This is the riskiest option for the consultant, who may never see any cash if the company does *not* prosper, yet it enables many companies to get the best advice possible when they need it most without depleting their thin capital resources.

## CHARGING FOR EXPENSES

Expenses incurred as a direct result of an assignment should be charged back to the client. Our usual direct client expenses include the following items:

- Telephone calls to or in behalf of the client.
- Reproduction costs (from an outside service, not our in-house costs).
- Overnight mail (not ordinary postage) charges.
- Materials (binders purchased, but not paper).
- Parking.
- Airplane or other public transportation costs.
- Subsistence (meals and hotels when on assignment).
- Mileage (at current accounting-approved rates).
- Books, software for the client, and similar other items, on a preapproved basis.

I cannot be earning full fees when I am stuck on the California freeways for two hours each way each day. Thus, although I normally prefer to charge for travel time, in a down economy and in public sector assignments, I find it difficult to negotiate our standard 50 percent of normal fee for travel time. But I note that clients are less likely to demand my presence whimsically for a fifteen-minute meeting or one that is canceled while I am en route when they have to pay the travel time involved.

## WHEN TO UP THE ANTE

Asking for a raise as an employee is simple compared to asking a client for an increase in fees. The request can be granted if you can show that you're getting decidedly below-market rates or if the tasks for which you are responsible have increased greatly.

I tend to have long-term relationships with our clients. The profitability of a long-term assignment can decrease markedly if you are absorbing overhead costs that have increased over that time—for example, when gas prices soared in the seventies, or postage rates increased, or telephone costs skyrocketed, or mandatory insurance increased. If you can pass those costs on to a client by your prior agreement as direct charges, then the major reasons left for increasing your fees are that your cost of living, along with everyone else's, has increased, or that demand for your services is so great that you are responding by increasing the price of your "supply."

I have a two-phase process for getting an increase in fees: I tear myself up inside for weeks or months before, and then finally meet with the client and discuss the increase. The former phase is painful, yet the latter is brief and pleasant each time I've done so. So why do I go through the first phase? While agonizing, I am putting myself in the client's position, trying to determine if there is enough justification from his or her perspective for an increase: importance of the project from here to the end; proof that he or she is underpaying me under current market conditions; and, of course, value received from my performance compared to alternatives. I then wait for the right moment to discuss fees—usually when I am handing an invoice over. I mention, at the end of the conversation, that we've been together a long time, and over that period the marketplace has increased its fees for the type of services I am providing, backed up by some professional statistics, and we are increasing our fee structure. I then give a letter summarizing the reasons for the increase, accompanied by the list of fees to be charged effective the next month, and indicate both on the fee structure sheet and during our conversation that we will continue to provide value at cost-effective fees and we appreciate the client's support and patronage.

Obviously, if you and your client do not have a robust relationship, this is not a good tactic to employ. You probably won't have a long-term relationship anyhow, so why terminate it sooner?

What if the client says no? Be prepared to be refused. Although this has not happened to me, I do prepare for it each time I've raised rates. Had a client balked, my strategy was to indicate a reduced level of commitment but with complete understanding for his or her position. But if *you've* done your homework, you already know that your client appreciates what you are doing, is committed to completion of the project, and feels he or she is being fair to you and that you are being fair as well. Our increases have been limited to 10 percent, and never more frequently than biannually.

On a short-term assignment, I suggest never raising rates. If you do so, probably you either did not estimate the fees properly in the first place or you are merely being greedy. If you end up renewing your agreement with the client, *then* you should negotiate a fee increase. But always remember to emphasize that increase in value you are providing, so the client feels he or she is still getting good value.

And a reminder: If you are not performing well, don't risk losing everything by asking for more. I am reminded of Dru, a subcontractor of ours whom we knew from a previous client. We were training him at our expense, and his hourly rate was more than he was worth from the outset. Twice during an eight-month period, he asked for increases, each of which I granted—for the wrong reasons. His performance was not good, but we felt it would take too much time to identify and train another resource in the time we had. Fifty thousand dollars later, little of the work Dru had done was usable. We had to pay again (from our own pockets) to redo nearly everything, this time properly. I have always been annoyed with myself that I compromised myself and my profits by allowing an increase to take effect without any increase in benefit. Clients I know feel the same about similar experiences.

# WHAT GOES UP MUST COME DOWN

If you can raise your fees, should you reduce them as well? If we go with the Keynesian model of supply and demand, when demand for your services decreases, should you lower your fees so that you can have sufficient work? If a task takes you so much less time than estimated and you are on a fixed-price assignment, do you go back to your client with a refund?

Because the economy is cyclical and demand varies, I have reconciled this issue by providing extra hours of consulting for our clients but not affecting the fee structure. Particularly with smaller clients, I have added a separate fee line on each invoice showing the number of hours provided at no charge—for example:

| | |
|---|---|
| 200 hours @ $175 per hour | $35,000 |
| 25 hours @ $0.00 per hour | 0 |

Clients appreciate this, and I have not committed myself to a lower rate, which then might have to be negotiated to a higher rate when the economy turns around. This solves a personal outlook: when I see additional work that needs to be done to ensure the project's success, I put the time in to do it rather than stop and negotiate a fee increase through a change order. Surely the client doesn't mind, and I don't mind either, because I feel my fee is a fair one to start with. That's the real meat of fee arrangements: If you do not feel it's fair, then it's not a good deal going in, and you should adjust the scope or the fees before you even start.

Often we as consultants have some on-the-job training. Should it be at the client's expense, or should we reduce fees or not charge? My position is that if it is one-time-only training mandatory to perform the assignment, I charge the client; if I can potentially use it elsewhere, I charge half; if it is not directly usable, I absorb the entire cost. In all cases, I try to have client personnel be part of any vendor-provided training, to ensure that the client has the potential for some internal capabilities after the assignment is complete.

## DOES ONE SIZE EVER FIT ALL? CHARGING AT VARIABLE RATES

Some consultants charge variable rates for what they are doing, often called *value pricing*, best illustrated by the joke about the consultant called in to fix a thorny problem in a continuous-process factory. The client quickly agreed to the $5,000 fee, which seemed small to correct a problem that had been evading solution for some time—and at great cost. The consultant goes in, ponders the situation, digs around, tweaks two valves, and—voilà—the problem is fixed in thirty minutes. The client is suddenly perturbed and says with astonishment to the consultant, "Why, that makes your effective rate $10,000 an hour. That's ridiculous!" To which the consultant replies: "My rate is merely $200 per hour. You simply paid $100 for the time, but $4,900 for me knowing where to look!"

And that is the essence of value consulting. If you have short-term specialty assignments, value consulting may be best for you. If you end up, as we do, with long-term assignments that encompass a variety of services we might provide during the term of the contract, value consulting is too complicated: How much is this service worth when I am wearing which hat?

Clients are willing to pay for instant response, your availability, your commitment over a period of time. You should charge for that. Not all clients need or want such responses. So when you are determining a fair rate, take into consideration the costs such an assignment will have on you personally before saying yes. Don't confuse value consulting with fair fee rates.

## PRESENTING THE BILL

In general, consultants do a poor job of making clients aware of the job they are doing for them. Perhaps it's the ingrained prejudice against advertising or touting our services, but it tends to work against us, so that when we present our bill to the client, there often is some question as to what we've done to warrant payment. One way of handling this is to "fold the ends of our toilet paper." Have you ever noticed the care with which the hotel maid bends down the ends of the toilet paper in your bathroom as she makes her presence and provision of service tangible to you? There is no overlooking the fact that she has been there and delivered her service.

The similarity between her services and ours as consultants is striking: We are decidedly in the service business ourselves, and there are *far too few tangibles to display for our clients.* Sure, we can wave a written proposal or report in front of our clients, or observe its presence on shelves, gathering the proverbial dust— testimony to money spent. But the real pith of what we deliver to our clients, regardless of our specialty area, contains much interim process work that is invisible to our client, such as developing support within the organization to facilitate the gathering of valid information, contacting vendors and researching via telephone, winning trust with both parties in warring factions that are ripping apart a client company, and monitoring the progress of the various parties internal and external to the client organization. So how can we bring our continuing interim efforts to our clients' attention?

First, *before you begin*, sit down with the client and explain what you will be doing—behind the scenes as well as in the forefront. Communicate what he or she can expect to see and expect to occur behind the scenes. Explain why these things need to be done.

Second, provide *ongoing status reports* to your client. These can be written or verbal, but above all make them concise, and build them in as part of any long-term assignment. Be aware that they can backfire if you put too much effort into them: Your client may think you're spending all of your time in paper folding and not in accomplishing the task.

Finally, *before you leave for the day*, ask yourself what you've communicated lately to your client. Perhaps a single telephone call or note left on the desk will prevent the anxiety or discontent that comes when there is no visible task progress.

We consultants *must* fold our paper ends through the use of the simplest method of all: communicating with our clients.*

I present the invoice in person, review it with my client, and make sure there are no unanswered questions or concerns. I always include a status report with the invoice as well, to indicate the tasks that have been performed, so the client knows what he or she has been getting for the money spent.

Sometimes it is not possible to present a final bill to a client: for example, when you are out of town on an assignment and finish before all of the expenses are known and can be invoiced. In that situation you can either submit a partial bill—for services to that point—when you leave, indicating that expenses will be billed separately, or send an invoice along later. If you do the latter, be sure to attach a personal note, to eliminate the harshness of a pristine bill.

---

*Reprinted from *Consultants News* (January 1988). © 1988 Kennedy Publications, Fitzwilliam, N. H.

# COLLECTING YOUR DUE

We all want to get paid for what we've done. We've usually spent a great deal of time preparing adequately for the assignment, with the proper letter of agreement, proposal, and execution. However, sometimes we simply have not been paid as agreed to. This is a thorny problem, because litigation against a client can deter future clients, regardless of how blameless we are.

You can prevent or at least substantially reduce revenue losses by checking credit on all new clients; stopping work if you are not paid within fifteen days (or thirty days, as agreed to in the contract and noted on each invoice); bill more frequently than monthly with new clients to determine how quickly they pay; or ask for an advance payment or retainer with new clients to ensure that they are sincere and will not be leaving you in the lurch.

Should a client be remiss in payment, call your counterpart in the client firm and have him or her resolve the delay. Sometimes the company is in dire trouble, and you'd best get your money out as quickly as you can; if the company ends up in bankruptcy, you'll be relegated to the typically long list of creditors, who may end up with nothing at all. Sometimes it's best to have a third party call and do the collections for you. I prefer this method where possible and appreciate the special talent of my office manager and right hand, Maxine, for doing so. Should there be some problem, the company is often more comfortable talking with her than embarrassing itself directly to me.

Sometimes a client just can't pay. Then it's best to take the loss as a bad debt and move on, wiser for the experience. If you have let that situation go to where you allowed the client to accumulate too many hours at your expense, then you've paid dearly for that experience.

# CHAPTER 5

---

# Marketing Your Consulting Expertise

**Y**ou cannot be a consultant, no matter how good, no matter how busy, over the long term without understanding the role of marketing in your business. And not only must you understand, but you must implement some marketing techniques, even subtly.

## MARKETING AND SALES

While this is not a primer on marketing and selling consulting services, no book on entry-level consulting would be complete without some mention of these activities, because marketing and selling are the life blood of consulting: You market your services and sell your solutions; if you don't, you will never have the opportunity to share your expertise and value with clients. (Refer to the Bibliography for a list of books devoted to specific selling techniques and issues.)

Although the terms frequently are used interchangeably, marketing and sales are *not* the same thing. Marketing encompasses the *strategy* of selling, and selling is the *tactics* you employ to get people to hire you (rather than another consultant). You should identify your marketing strategy before you try to sell to the firms you've targeted. Mickey Rosenau used to differentiate between them as follows during seminars. He'd take a $10 bill and show it to those assembled: "I can sell this bill to any of you here for $10; but as a marketer I could convince you that this *particular* bill that I'm now holding has such intrinsic value and worth that you'd be willing to pay me $20 for it." And that's a critical difference, in both perception and in our income stream. Since consulting is a profession with remarkably few barriers to entry and to exit, the onus is on you to convince your prospects that *your* particular consulting service—not someone else's—has intrinsic value for their businesses.

I have found that volunteer work in professional associations has been a good marketing strategy for me. I have used the contacts gleaned there to identify potential opportunities, which I then follow up with sales literature identifying our capabilities in the subject area rather than make a cold call. I do not enjoy cold calls and therefore do not come across as well when I try to make them. Also, because I have a hearing problem, I am less comfortable when making telephone calls than I am face to face. The professional association encounters allow me to know my sales target rather well and to sell myself over a longer period of time, and more subtly, than other methods.

For example, in our field, construction management information systems, the potential client firms have in-house staffs that can handle small projects on a part-time basis. When a very large construction job presents itself, they usually do not have the information technology staff available to assess the requirements of that particular project. Thus, we direct our sales thrust to the construction management firms that have public sector clients with very large jobs. We supplement one another rather than compete.

Your professional involvement is best done in a related field. For example, I have been active nationally and locally in the Construction Management Association of America (CMAA), as well as in management consulting organizations, because I get to know our target market better. But if you do get involved in an organization, you *must* perform whatever volunteering you do as you do a client assignment, and well, or your marketing attempts will backfire.

If you want your clients to be at the top level in organizations— say, CEO level—then your goal will not best be served by going to middle management organizations. You'd best attend Kiwanis or Lions or Rotary meetings.

I also know extremely successful consultants who can promote themselves through a telephone line. Whatever works for *you* is what counts. And not all techniques are going to work as well for every individual. The important part is to try some of the approaches and then figure out what seems to be your best way of approaching prospects and converting them into clients.

Dave Norris, one of the first consultants I met, had a funnel approach to the consultants' sales cycle: ensure that the *suspects* from the universe as a whole come into the funnel at the widest end, are qualified into *prospects*, and then are converted into *clients*. The challenge is to keep the funnel filled, because once they get into the wide end, the mathematics of the process should result in the development of enough clients.

Identify in your marketing assessment:

- The industry you wish to serve.
- The type(s) of services you wish to provide.
- The individuals who make the decisions to acquire those services in that industry.

- The competition and its strength and weakness.
- That a marketplace exists for your services.

## MARKETING TACTICS

Once you've targeted your market, you can identify which tactics will best reach it. The following sections discuss the pros and cons of various marketing tactics.

## Cold Calls

These leave *me* cold. I feel about them somewhat the same as going to mixers for other single people when I was in college. I recall with no fondness those awkward moments on the telephone, or in person, when the other party doesn't seem to be at all interested in anything but getting rid of me. I've made a few of these calls, mostly early on in my practice before I knew how to prequalify prospects. I now use the telephone and the exchange of written materials before I venture out to see someone, because of the costly nature of the service we offer. The reengineering or automation of an entire company is not a spontaneous decision.

Bob Kahn, a successful retailing management consultant, always stated that he'd made only one cold call in fifty-three years of consulting, and he sustained an active and successful practice.

To whom do you make a cold call? After all, if you don't know them (the definition of a cold call), how do you find out about them? You can research data from libraries and industry magazines, buy names from lists through the many services that maintain them, or check the want ads in the newspapers to see who is in need of which services. But remember that other consultant hopefuls are

102

also using these same sources, so your approach must be different enough to make you stand out in what might well be a crowd.

## Telemarketing

I consider telemarketing (to the dismay of the professional telemarketers, I'm sure) merely a more contemporary version of the cold call. Since *I* find them obtrusive and turn-offs rather than turn-ons, I avoid the technique. But I do know consultants who have successfully used it to get new business. They hire a telemarketing company that does the calling, and from the calls placed a few interviews are scheduled, at which the consultant can show his or her wares. Sometimes a prospect becomes a client; more often than not, not.

## Newsletters

The old story is that dog bites man is not news, but when man bites dog, there's news! I know many consultants who write successful newsletters but no successful consultants who buy a newsletter from a distributor and then send it out under the consultant's name. If you decide you must have a newsletter, write it yourself or have it written under your direction—and make it unique. After all, you're trying to differentiate yourself from other consultants, so why take the risk of sounding like others?

I receive numerous newsletters from others, and the best ones are brief, specific, and reflective of the writer. (There are many books written on how to write newsletters; see the sources in the Bibliography.)

Note that newsletters do not apply to everything or suit everyone. For someone with many smaller clients who share a common interest—say, retailing—Bob Kahn's industry newsletter brings information not readily obtained. However, for data processing consultants who work on multiyear assignments for a single client on special-purpose tasks of narrow interest range, there may not be much newsworthy.

Another question to ask yourself when contemplating a newsletter is this: Would you find it interesting if it came in your mailbox? If not, don't send it.

## Public Speaking

Some consultants I know are incredibly good public speakers. They appear to talk effortlessly before an assembled multitude, while I have come to know my speaking gremlins on a first-tremor basis by now. (In fact, when I don't feel the butterflies starting to flap their wings in my stomach, I worry.) But after decades I've discovered that those slick speakers actually practice as much as I do and have their own gremlins to deal with; they just look as though they don't. And therein lies a secret: If you can plan ahead to control the environment as much as possible, you'll feel more comfortable. And, of course, you should know what you're talking about.

I had occasion to work with Somers White, the consummate speaker in management consulting. Beforehand, I had always perceived him as slick. He never stumbled over a word or phrase, he modulated his voice so that not one person in the room lost interest, and he made what was hard for me look effortless. But I discovered through our joint effort that he:

- Planned early on what he was going to say.
- Followed up repeatedly to eliminate potential last-minute speaker questions.

- Visited the facility well before the meeting and dealt with the facility staff to ensure that the room and stage were precisely as he wanted them to be.

In other words, he left as little to chance as was possible. His focus was therefore entirely on the performance. And was he ever impressive!

## Articles

If you write well, articles published in periodicals where your potential clients will read them can be a source of credibility, enhancing your chances of getting assignments. They are relatively inexpensive to reproduce and can make excellent enclosures when sending an introductory package to a prospect. You can also leave them as handouts at seminars or meetings you attend. But you can spend a great deal of time trying to get your articles placed in periodicals— time that you might better spend on billable client assignments.

Try collaborating with a client on an article. It's a wonderful opportunity to get valuable time with a client and associate your name with an industry leader. I've collaborated with clients on articles in our field of construction management, for example.

When you reproduce your articles, you can merely take them down to your local copy store or even use your own copier, but using glossy paper with a professional-looking border creates a better image. If you amass a group of articles, I suggest you do what I did, which ended up saving postage on mailings and improved my image. After many years and many articles, I had quite a package of reprints to send to prosepcts. One day I happened to see the hefty package and decided to put on my "recipient's" hat. What I saw bothered me: Some articles were old; some of the concepts in some articles were outdated; some of the articles were very much alike. As a result, I stopped sending more than three articles, unless specifically requested by a prospect to do so. The pressure is on me, now, however, because I haven't been writing for a while, and my storehouse is getting empty.

## Mass Mailings

Would *you* buy a critical service based on a minimal-postage piece that appeared unsolicited? Highly doubtful, unless you were getting something very important from the mailer—which is even more doubtful because the decision makers I know throw (or have their secretaries throw) such mail into the circular file immediately. If you are selling a seminar, book, or other product, this technique can be useful, especially when you purchase a targeted mailing list, but it is not a productive technique for consultants.

*Consultants' News* puts a rule of thumb for mass mailings at 10,000 pieces, generating 200 inquiries, resulting in 1 client. It advises, "The more targeted the mailing and the more defined the message, the greater the response and chance of success. And . . . a mailing without follow-up is wasted money."*

If you do decide to try this tactic, pay attention to the mailing lists that you use. These lists are not all the same. Typically we pay more attention to the materials we enclose rather than the hit rate of a particular list. For example, some companies update their lists more frequently, so the names and addresses are more current. Count your conversions from using these lists, not merely the numbers of inquiries. For example, you might get lots of inquiries that merely tie you up while you could be generating leads resulting in actual conversions—a better use of *your* time.

*Reprinted from *Consultants News* (January 1993). © 1993 Kennedy Publications, Fitzwilliam, N. H.

## Yellow Pages

Would *you* buy a critical service from the telephone directory? In all my years of consulting, I've had only one job that came from a Yellow Pages ad contributed to by the local Los Angeles Association of Management Consultants members years ago. The company's purchasing agent contacted me because he used the Yellow Pages frequently to identify vendors. The assignment itself was not very satisfying because he was too low in the organization to gain the support he (and I) needed. Still, some consultants swear by that medium. Whether it is useful to you probably depends highly on your functional specialty area, your geographic area, and your client base's traditional source of vendors.

What I did get from Yellow Pages ads, however, was a steady stream of résumés from consultant wanna-bes, that, despite three moves continues unabated. Oh, and I did stop the Yellow Pages ads over a decade ago!

## Other Advertising

You can place advertisements in local business journals, trade magazines, and various community booklets. However, this kind of passive advertising is useful only if you can truly generate business with it. I have not found it at all fruitful. Many years ago I even placed an ad in the *Wall Street Journal's* special section of data processing, generating dozens of résumés but not a single inquiry. I never did that again, because the ad itself was so costly.

You could go to trade shows, although in consulting it's hard to have a glitzy booth that competes well with booths of product vendors. I believe it works well for the computer hardware and software vendors I know but not for consultants.

Finally, you can get free listings in directories of consultants. I've been in business for so long that I am on many mailing lists and frequently get letters asking me to review my complimentary listing in this or that "elite" directory. I can honestly say that I've never received a single inquiry from the dozens of listings that must exist out there by now, so those directories must be so very elite that not even my marketplace can access them! And yes, I probably do get many résumés because of those listings.

# Referrals

There's nothing quite like a referral from a peer to a potential client—except perhaps a referral from a prior client to a potential client. People do not refer those they do not respect and esteem to those they know. So in a way, referral can be viewed as a double compliment: esteem for the job you did and respect for you as an individual. It is another way of saying they'd hire you again if they had the chance.

When you have been referred, you have a leg up in the process of winning the assignment. Because you have someone in common, you are on more comfortable footing than if you were making a cold call. In essence, by getting your foot in the door through the third-party introduction, you can start your discussions on a more targeted level. Because you know the individual opposite you is interested in buying, the sales environment for you is better.

Don't forget to ask your peer or former client who did the referring whatever you need to gain the background to prepare you for your meeting or call with the prospect. And, above all, regardless of how the encounter turns out, *send a thank-you note for the referral.* Reinforced behavior is repeated behavior, and certainly you want repeated referrals.

Since referrals are such a productive source of business, you need to maximize them. First, as Bob Kahn always has said, "If I don't know you, how can I refer you?" Network as much as you can—not working the room in the obvious and sometimes crass way that can put others off but just getting out there and meeting new people. Explain what you do; listen to their explanations of what they do. If there appears to be a common ground, explore it over time. I won't recommend a flash-in-the-pan consultant, but I am delighted to recommend someone who has sustained his or her practice over time and is professional in demeanor and appearance.

Professional meetings, alumni events, and community volunteer activities are all sources of potential clients for you.

## Seminars

I know of a number of consultants who are proficient in presenting seminars for targeted client groups. They maintain a mailing list of target executives, pay for their attendance at these seminars, and offer a free lunch as well. This can be an expensive way to woo clients, but it tends to be successful in obtaining clients from the prospect pool.

When you host seminars, properly target the attendees, so that the subject matter will be perceived as worth their investment of time, and be sure everything is done in a first-class manner—from the facility where you hold the event, to the materials, to the invitations—so you impart that important image of professionalism.

Sometimes you can team with a third party who is willing to foot the bill for such a seminar, and from which you can get a pool of prospects from which to work. But be careful that you don't ally yourself with the wrong third party, to the detriment of your image of impartiality.

# Teaching

If you have the requisite credentials and are good at doing so, teaching courses, especially in colleges for working adults, might generate business for you. It is, however, a grueling and not always productive method. And if you find yourself traveling frequently, the stress of having to find substitute teachers might not be worth the effort.

# Personal Communication

If mass techniques don't apply, then how best can you reach people? I can't emphasize enough the value of a personal note when you see an article of interest or, better, an article featuring someone you know or something you know to be of interest. I generally cut out the article and send it to the recipient with a note of congratulations. Remember the personal things the client may have mentioned: birthdays, graduations, sports interests in the family, bereavements. Of course, none of these things will or can work if the task performance is not credible.

Don't forget to include lunches and breakfasts as a way to extend yourself. If you find yourself in another city, make an opportunity to meet a client you may not otherwise get to. Although it's a cold call, it's a bit warmer because the fact that you happen to be in the neighborhood gives you a reason to call—and more likelihood that you can get to the prospect if he or she is interested in your services.

Volunteerism also comes under the category of a personal selling tactic, but be sure to do a superb job as a volunteer. If you make a poor impression by not being responsive or responsible when you've committed to volunteer, it's highly doubtful that you'll be contacted to do business later.

Although we all have to balance volunteer commitments against the financial requirements of a fee-for-service business, there are professional benefits from becoming involved. For example, chairing committees nationally and running programs locally help you learn from others and fine-tune your organizational and management skills while you gain the satisfaction of accomplishing something that benefits others. We have a responsibility to give a bit of ourselves and our time to ensure that our profession keeps its standards high and that our needs are not ignored by other interests.

## PUBLIC RELATIONS

Public relations (PR) is the process of getting yourself known in the field in which you consult. Getting your name out there can consist of interviews, articles written by you or quoting you, or public speaking. You can do some PR yourself, but there are individuals and firms specializing in it, and these firms can usually do a much more effective job than you can, because they are in contact with the media for all of their clients and can identify opportunities. Remember that you're in the consulting business and should be spending your time on marketing and delivering services to clients.

PR will not get you business directly, but it will make prospects familiar with your name and the services you provide—in a favorable manner. I know many successful consultants who have paid liberally over the years for PR campaigns of their practices and cannot directly connect any one single engagement to that cost. However, the intangible aspects of image development contribute indirectly to every assignment we win.

Consultants seem to have a difficult time promoting themselves. They generally eschew the snake oil salesman approach and try to stay above selling. Yet creating an image of competence can be helped by the appearance of your name in a local newspaper with a sage quotation. Being quoted as an authority on a subject can help make you that authority!

How can you best do PR? Wherever you spot an opportunity, exploit it yourself, but don't ignore the professional PR firm. The latter is not cheap, and you need to commit for a year to have a remote chance of seeing results. I used a PR specialist for nearly two years. As a result, I had many reproducible articles in a variety of professional and general business periodicals, I made radio and television appearances, and I was called frequently for an expert opinion. I did not obtain any clients as a direct result of the PR campaign, but the materials developed and the contacts with the media did strengthen my reputation for a number of years. But image created by PR is perishable, and experts in my field, technology, are also perishable because the technology changes so rapidly. I'm about ready to retain that same firm again, though I could go directly to the media. The firm handles all of the inquiries, hears the noes and follows the yesses, and, most important, keeps my focus on the writing and media contact, which is important to differentiate me from the pack of other consultants.

Unless you have a great deal of excess capital, you're best off waiting until you've got a few assignments under your belt and you have both the funds and the experience to share with readers before you spend money on a PR campaign. And as part of your marketing campaign, you can attend to the following PR elements yourself:

- Where and how professional your offices appear.
- How your telephone is answered.
- The impression your stationery and written materials create.
- How you communicate—the tone and the timeliness of response.

- How much you charge and how it relates to others' fee structures.
- Your own appearance.*

Be sure that the image you *do* create is a consistent one.

Should you have the opportunity to work directly with the press (which I do *not* advocate if you can afford to pay a professional to do so), be open and honest, but *do* be careful about whom you're talking with. I have often asked the interviewer to send me a copy of the article prior to publication so that I can review it for accuracy, but most reporters are working with a tight deadline, and most media do *not* allow this. Try to be quotable, using clear, brief, targeted phrases that have analogies most people can relate to. A good idea is to keep written notes of the conversation so that you can follow up with the reporter to ensure that you see the article or quotation when the article appears. It's somewhat embarrassing to have clients calling you about an article in which you stated something but you have absolutely no idea of what it might be!

If you are called by a reporter and are not able to help, refer that person to someone else. Reporters appreciate this, as does the referred. Once I referred someone who was better qualified than I was in the subject area for an article in the *Wall Street Journal*. It generated significant interest and many inquiries and got her business off to a flying start.

Should you decide to write an article for a periodical, be sure that you make it something of use to the readers and to the editors of that publication. For example, how-to articles, say, on computer selection, are generally more helpful than a theoretical discussion of computer chips.

*Reprinted from *Consultants News*, Special Reports (October 1991). © 1991 Kennedy Publications, Fitzwilliam, N.H.

You could prepare your own press kit rather than have a professional do it for you. Include the following:

- A fact sheet, which contains your biography, what you do briefly described (capabilities), and a brief description of what makes *your* firm unique or special.
- List of publications and tapes.
- List of seminars or talks you give.
- List of areas on which you are an expert (but be sure you really are *expert* in these areas).
- Case studies and/or reprints of articles, if applicable.
- A black-and-white photograph of yourself.

Specify the person to call about more information and the address and telephone number.

You could also include a press release on a topic of interest for use by the media, but if you are going to go to the trouble of preparing the press kit, you'll also need to follow it up with telephone calls to ensure that the recipients received it and remember you (favorably of course!). You should distribute it with a cover letter suggesting some immediate use to which the editor might put the kit, and you should update it every six months or so. As you can see, it's a lot of work for you to do.

## SOME COMMON STRATEGIES

I cannot emphasize enough the understanding of the importance of your marketing strategy before you embark on selling yourself. Without a strategy, you'll end up spending considerable effort and money in fruitless activities that hinder you from, rather than help you toward, achieving your goal. The reader is referred to books written on marketing consulting services in the Bibliography for a more complete treatment of this all-important topic.

Briefly, strategies often are market oriented (which sector of the market do you plan to address, public or private?); others, organizational (joint venture with another company or alone?); others, based on pricing (go for pieces of the complete task because budget is available incrementally?); or, product oriented (associate with a vendor's product or product line?). When you evaluate marketing strategies, there are always pros and cons associated with each one. Some of the more common trade-offs you must make are shown in Exhibit 5-1.

## MARKETING IN A SLOW ECONOMY

When work becomes scarce and the wolves are at your door, what can you do? Should you change your marketing strategy or techniques during the inevitable downturns on the economy? Other than redoubling your efforts and keeping in touch with clients who may be having as difficult a time as you are, there's not much else you can do. It helps to differentiate yourself, if you can, from your competition, and keep yourself visible. The downturns always bottom out, and you want to be first in line to get the business that results when the economy turns.

The poor-economy wolf is not to be confused, however, with the howling wolf due to the passing of your particular specialty fad. The marketplace is still there; it's your services that are no longer required. When the economy gets better, you still won't have a market for your services. You've just become a dinosaur and need to reevaluate what you are doing and will do in the future as a consultant.

**Exhibit 5-1**

EVALUATING MARKETING STRATEGIES

| Strategy | Pros | Cons |
|---|---|---|
| Public sector | Long-term, allowing you to plan; minority business enterprise (MBE), disadvantaged business enterprise (DBE), and women business enterprise (WBE) advantages. | Heavy administrative overhead; long lead times between bid and award; long payment cycle; lower fees than private sector. |
| Public and trade awareness | Your expertise is known to your marketplace. | If industry is in decline, you will be too; conflicts of interest can arise more easily. |
| Joint ventures and alliances | You can ally yourself with well-known companies. | You lose your visibility and independence. |
| Project pricing (vs. T&M) | Easier to bill, often easier to sell to a client. | If you misjudge, can be highly unprofitable. |
| Network with vendors of related products | They market for you and prequalify prospects. | If they fall into disfavor, so do you; especially in technical areas, you can lose your expertise and market. |

# MARKETING TO YOUR PEERS

There are two prime sources of work: your client base (past and future clients) and your peers (other consultants). Since you never quite know who might be a future client or a potential source for future clients, everyone conceivably is in either one or the other group, and therefore you should be sure you come across in a way that fosters confidence in you and your professionalism.

We often get so involved in directing our marketing efforts to our potential clients that we forget the other side of the consultant's two-sided marketing thrust: marketing to our peers. Peer referrals have a higher hit ratio; after all, you've been referred by an already trusted consultant, and the client has expressed interest just by contacting you. What a nice way to narrow down the potential marketplace for your services!

What prompts peer referral? First, of course, is your expertise in a specialty needed by someone's existing client—either in a non-competitive field or to supplement someone's own services. Second, but more important, are the three aspects of professionalism; internal (by quality of expression, written and oral), external (how you dress and behave), and your contribution to the consulting profession in terms of books, articles, and relevant experience. Repeated peer referrals come from performing satisfactorily on the client's behalf, reflecting well on the recommending consultant.

How do you market to your peers? First, no one can refer you if they don't know who you are and what you are doing—now, not years ago. So keep your peers informed as to your current assignments and interest. Second, get together with these peers at professional meetings. And finally, impress your peers with your consulting competence rather than your salesmanship—and perhaps they'll soon be doing the marketing for you.

# EFFECTIVE NETWORKING

I view networking as the process of circulating among professional and personal venues with the goal of getting to know others and letting them get to know you so that some future mutual opportunities might develop—the peer group interaction that leads to connecting us all. You can network through informal groups, formal meetings of professional associations, and one-on-one encounters.

Networking can increase your marketing capability as others get to know what you can do for them, and it also can increase your capability to deliver services by letting you know others who can help you on client assignments. Networking also allows you to:

- Find out what's happening with competitors.
- Find out what's happening in your client base industry.
- Get new ideas by reacting to and with others (synergy).
- Learn more about market trends.

The best networkers I know are good at expressing themselves: They can "work the room" and effectively communicate what it is they do and how they can benefit you. Networking is a two-stage process, and it is a continuing effort. The first stage is to meet someone; the second stage consists of following up that meeting with a reminder that you are still there. A common misconception is that the initial meeting is all you need. But if you follow up meetings with letters, articles, and telephone calls that are tastefully done and well received, you've developed a relationship that can help you: with a collegial referral (by a peer) or a client referral.

## CATCHING WORK OVERFLOW

Depending on where you are located and your specialty area, often you can profit professionally and financially from the opportunity to assist a colleague with his or her surplus business. In fact, many consultants got their start here in southern California from the overflow needs created by the burgeoning aerospace business. (Of course, as the aerospace business shrunk, many consultants found themselves without marketplaces.)

This opportunity is much like being a subcontractor. The advantages to assisting, as many fine surgeons do during complex operations requiring the expertise of more than one physician, is that all of the overhead is assumed by the prime consultant and you have no marketing requirements. But the assisting person loses control over the scheduling, the fees, and the solution implemented. If you don't mind giving control to someone else to have a robust market for your services, then hook yourself to another's star.

Assisting is also a way to get started in consulting and keep yourself from starving. Of course, if you later have an opportunity to consult as the prime yourself, be sure to honor commitments you've already made to the sponsoring consultant. Above all, since you'll probably end up in competition with your former referral source, be sure to avoid bad-mouthing him or her. As they say in football, "Don't forget the ones who've brung you."

## BEING A SUBCONTRACTOR

Over the years, I've employed many subcontractors because different clients have different needs and the technology we use to satisfy those needs changes rapidly. I've also been a subcontractor to other consultants. In both roles, I've learned that being the best subcontractor is not the same as being the best consultant. Most consultant attributes are the same—doing a good job, identifying potential opportunities, charging only for time worked, and keeping good records—but there is one attribute missing in many consultants that is mandatory for being a good subcontractor: taking direction from someone else.

When you work for another consultant, you go in under that person's umbrella: his or her name, criteria, objectives. Thou shalt not:

- Woo his or her clients for yourself.
- Compromise the other consultant for the client.
- Discuss money with the client unless instructed to do so (and how).
- Discuss contractual issues with the client.
- Speak for the consultant unless instructed to do so (and how).

Thou shalt:

- Represent yourself as part of the consultant's organization.
- Refer problems and opportunities to the consultant immediately.
- Act in every regard as a good employee of the consultant.
- Suppress your own ego.

The dialectic in subcontracting is that you've probably gone into consulting so that you don't have to take direction from someone else, yet as a subcontractor ("sub"), you've introduced one more layer of direction-giving to your task performance, and that means at least one more layer of politics with which to deal.

The advantages to subcontracting are many, however. You are not responsible for the ongoing marketing, billing, administration, and risk that the prime consultant assumes. You have the best of both situations: You can work more autonomously than an employee, but your income is assured by the prime consultant, who, by running the organization, allows you to perform the task you best like. Be sure to sign an agreement, such as the Subcontractor Letter of Agreement in Exhibit 3-6, to articulate your specific arrangements.

I have subs with whom I've worked for over a decade. They are characterized by honesty, good attitudes, good work, and reliability. I use them wherever I can because they add to the capabilities I offer; they do not sap my already limited resources.

As I've matured in consulting I've realized that *my* subcontracting abilities needed refinement and have tried to suppress my own ego and ensure that the prime contractor deals with the client on substantive issues—even if I have identified the solution. The client has hired the prime, not me. I expect my subs to manifest the same consideration.

Not all issues should be handled by subs. Clients who ask how much something will cost to do should be referred to the prime. Subs can estimate hours if the prime has so approved, or the sub can get back to the client after checking with the prime. But if a sub specifies a dollar amount or a number of hours that does not include the analysis or other time the prime must put into the task, he or she has established an awkward situation where the client's expectation is for a far lower fee than has been quoted.

Additionally, if as a sub the client asks, "How much do you get paid?"—and then possibly offers you an assignment directly—just indicate to the client you're uncomfortable discussing such items; these are matters for the prime. This is an awkward situation, but if you regard subcontracting as the best of all possible assignments, you have to subjugate your desire to give a complete and direct answer to the business needs of the prime. The best rule of thumb is, "Loose lips sink ships." A prime who feels unsure of how you'll react in this sort of situation will be reluctant to put you in that situation.

One subcontractor we had was energetic and sharp, but reminded me more of a loose cannon than a consultant. He meant well but talked before he thought, and at no point (it seemed) did his brain contribute to his lips' output. For example, when a client was cutting back on the coffee allocated to the project, he was boasting of his expense account and ability to eat out anywhere and stay at a hotel of his choice. If asked if something could be done, he always said yes, making the client respond when I said no, "But *he* said he'd do it." Sigh.

Remember, your role as a sub is to *enhance* the prime's effectiveness with the client, not subvert it.

I've evolved the 3 A.M. rule: If I continue to wake up at three in the morning worried about what a sub is going to do, then I know that sub is not for me. I sever the relationship rather than continue to take the risk and lose the sleep.


## MOONLIGHT OR LIMELIGHT?

The easiest way to ease yourself into consulting is often to consult part-time while continuing with your present full-time job. The advantage is that you don't leave a secure environment for one you would not have liked anyhow. The disadvantage is that it's not truly a test: You aren't submerging yourself into the insecurity of having to support yourself entirely on others' whims, while you are working very hard.

Many consultant wanna-bes have become wazwuns quickly. Lured by the appeal of all the assignments that they were offered when working for someone else, they quickly discovered that they were not remunerative or frequent enough to cover expenses when the "real" job went away.

I've occasionally used moonlighters as subcontractors, but they uniformly did not work out well, for the following reasons. First, a moonlighter is generally unavailable during the day, when the client wants to see him or her. Second, moonlighters often are fatigued mentally, not to mention physically, and they make more mistakes, at least in my experience, than their full-time consulting counterparts. While we're deep into an era of telecommuting and to some degree teleconsulting as well, there are occasions when the consulting presence is needed on-site and fully alert. Third, I want to be sure that my consultants are going to be available in the future, and although there's no assurance that any subcontractor *will* be there, I take more seriously those who have made a more permanent commitment to the consulting profession.

Be aware, then, that moonlighting to test the waters is not a fair test because you place tremendous pressure on yourself. You might not perform as well under moonlighting as you would when you are less fatigued. You must decide if you can handle multiple demands simultaneously and often asynchronously. If you need little sleep and perform consistently well, then moonlighting might suit you and your biorhythms.

# CHAPTER 6

---

# How to Sell

**T**here never can be too much written about selling. Above all, you must distinguish between selling and marketing, as noted in Chapter 5. Although they are very much intertwined, marketing is concerned with creating the demand for your extraordinary services, which is of no great value if you don't learn how to close the sale. Again, I refer you to the excellent books devoted specifically to selling consulting services, listed in the Bibliography, but will just note a few of the items here that I think consultants must master.

## SELLING YOURSELF IS LIKE SELLING YOUR CAR

Please understand that I, too, feel that my expertise and experience are so valuable, so important, that they should not have to be relegated to the crass sales techniques used by used car salespeople.

Prospects should be beating down my door and crowding my telephone lines because my CV (curriculum vitae) speaks for itself. But unless I tout my capabilities, how can a potential client differentiate me from the masses of other consultants out there? Remember when professionals did not advertise? Those days of professional smugness are gone—probably forever—as doctors, dentists, lawyers, *and consultants* advertise in the media.

Selling ourselves is like selling a car, for two reasons. Compare the sales techniques used by luxury car salespeople to those used by the used car salespeople. When you go to your Lexus dealer as a prospect, you get coffee, private offices, and a broad range of services added to the basic car being sold: free loaner cars when your car needs servicing, free pickup if your car breaks down. When you go to Al's Used Car Mart, what you see is really all you get, and Al doesn't have much more to sell other than the hulks you see on the lot. If Al spent the money for marketing that Lexus did, he'd have a broader range of clients to keep him busy. Lexus is not selling—they're creating an aura of elegance as their marketing strategy, and everything they do in their sales process supports that image; their marketing helps them make easier sales to the right people.

So when you go to meet a prospect, you can offer the client a broader range of services in addition to the basic assignment. I had an interim management assignment where I was responsible for managing a division of a company, turning around the nonperforming unit, and then hiring a replacement for myself. I built into the assignment a follow-up visit ninety days and six months after my departure so that I could evaluate how well the division was performing and thus ensure that the unit was not exhibiting signs of recidivism. I would have kept in touch with the client anyhow, but this was a formal part of the assignment that indicated my commitment to the client after my tenure had ended. There was no additional charge for those visits.

Second, the salesperson, no matter what type of car you are buying, will talk up the benefits you'll reap by buying his or her car. The salesperson wants to come to closure quickly rather than lose the sale. The chances of making the sale, despite what you say, decrease greatly once you walk out of the showroom, so the salesperson addresses your concerns constructively, whether they be of financing, size, color, or performance, and tells you how much better the vehicle you're looking at is than the competition's. The best salespeople do the comparison in terms of what it means to you as the buyer, based on reinforcement from all the media advertising of the car's features: gas savings (if you're concerned about ongoing costs), size (if, like me, you're daunted by the prospect of fitting a large car into micro-spaces now in vogue in parking lots), service needs (if you're put off by spending too much of your time in service departments), and reliability (if you are dismayed by the risk of spending your time waiting for tow trucks on freeways when you should be at a client meeting).

Now reread the previous paragraph, and substitute the benefits your prospective client could reap from your services—and you've just made a sales presentation. Remember, if you can't sell yourself, your client won't buy.

## THE SALES MODEL

Consulting is not a product usually bought sight unseen, so, above all, you need to get to the potential client. Dave Norris, one of the longest practicing management consultants in California, talks of potential clients as suspects, who are qualified into prospects, and delightedly, finally winnowed into clients. My model addresses the processes of generating clients in terms of successive activities:

$$qualify \rightarrow introduce \rightarrow propose \rightarrow close \rightarrow perform$$

Once you've identified the groups who are *qualified* to be your clients (say, through professional associations, industry lists, for example), you must *introduce* yourself and your capabilities to them. If that introduction reveals a valid task you can perform for the individual and/or the company, you may prepare and submit a *proposal.* However, not every proposal is accepted, and you must *close* the sale. Finally, no amount of salesmanship can overcome work that is not carried out well. So, *performance* is the final step in your sales process. You can propose additional work, of course, as shown above, after you've performed assignments for clients. You've already prequalified them and introduced yourself, so you can propose and close on repeat work.

## QUALITY, *NOT* QUANTITY

One of the common mistakes fledgling (and experienced) consultants make is viewing the number of contacts with the customer world as selling. However, it's not the *quantity* of contacts you make but the *quality* of each contact that matters. I can go through every office within a twenty-story building talking to the office manager, but if the offices are for physicians and I specialize in consulting to warehouses, I am spinning my wheels with very little chance of success. So the first thing to do is to ensure that the individual(s) you have targeted are in a business in which you have expertise of value and are high enough in the organization or in the right department to appreciate your talents and either introduce you to the individuals who *do* authorize your services or authorize themselves.

If you can get some background information on the firm, you might be able to find out about pending projects or events that would make what you have to sell of greater and more immediate value, but often you can't do that beforehand. So you have a true purpose in this initial meeting: qualifying whether the company has an immediate need for your services.

The actual qualification of the individual can be done by telephone or in person, although using the telephone and some follow-up correspondence is often the best way to use your limited time. Over the years, the true potential clients seem to exhibit the following characteristics, which I've identified as "Marsha's Five Signs of a Real Prospect":

1. Immediate need.
2. Available funding.
3. High priority to task.
4. Sponsor high in the organization.
5. Palpable chemistry.

The first four signs are logical and can be clearly determined and then evaluated. It's the fifth that makes an assignment—makes it go well and makes it enjoyable. It may be the glint in the eyes, a common basis for discussion, personableness, or some unquantifiable energy that I look for when I'm meeting a potential client. I feel as though this person wants to work with me as I wish to work with him or her.

Put aside for a moment the desire to close a sale and reflect on the individual you met with. Does this person seem genuine? Sincere? Did you get a strong sense of unspoken but obvious hidden agendas? Can you imagine yourself sitting with him or her and delivering a highly difficult report on findings? Would he or she be the type who shoots the messenger—and if so, do you want to be part of that scenario? The questions you can ask go on and on, but the purpose is to reflect a moment on the chemistry in addition to the factual basis of the meeting before proceeding.

I've had few assignments I didn't like, but those that stand out as mismatches were clear cases of missing chemistry. One client micromanaged the project to the extent that I spent more time on reporting how time was being spent than on consulting. He knew it but was more interested in controlling the project very closely. I felt that there was little that could be comfortably accomplished, and we did not continue together for long. Another client was so disinterested in the assignment that there was no challenge in making anything at all happen.

Disinterest and micromanagement alone are not signs of probably ungratifying assignments, but they contribute to the sense of chemistry. Had I followed my intuition in both cases, I would not have pursued the assignment. Sometimes money alone is not enough to make an assignment tolerable.

## "WITH WHOM DO I HAVE THE PLEASURE?"

The initial meeting with your potential client is fraught with perils. You usually have two to three minutes to become comfortable enough to make this person want to hire you—if not right now, then as soon as possible—because you've convinced him or her of your intrinsic worth to the organization. That's a pretty large order and can best be accomplished if your meeting isn't being constantly interrupted by telephone calls or employees with crises. Getting him or her out of the office, say at a professional association meeting, is often fraught with others vying for attention. So what's a consultant to do?

I see the initial meeting as having the primary purpose of introducing me to the prospective client and the client and his business to me. I am not interested in a hard sale approach at this point, because I've found that separating the introductory phase from the selling phase enables us to get to know one another better. Having said that, of course, if you have been called in by a prospect, you are essentially preintroduced, and the goal of the initial meeting is then to arrive at the possibility of a suitable proposal being generated.

I prefer to meet prospective clients at their place of business. It gives me insight into their management styles, their corporate values, and the products or services being sold. Scanning the site enables me to see whether dark-paneled walls and leather-bound reports are the norm, or if shirtsleeves and bulletized delivery are the norm. That helps me better price out what I eventually propose: I can allocate time and money for the expensive binding, without which some clients won't value the findings.

When setting up the initial meeting, I am hoping that we get to know one another—our needs, areas in common, and potential for the future. That relieves the pressure of having to close in fifteen minutes, which is the amount of time I aim for. Rarely does it end in fifteen minutes, but if there is little in common, we've no need to go on much longer. I am attempting only to introduce myself and my services and to learn about this prospect. I have found that it's even easier to get an appointment when the other party feels I'm not trying to sell anything, merely to introduce myself and get to know him or her better should a need arise at some future time. I want this prospective client to understand that I am completely committed to and enthusiastic about him or her, the company, and the project.

## LISTEN WHILE YOU LEARN

The best way to qualify is to listen to the other person: how he or she perceives the business and his or her role in it, the business's role in the community, and perhaps your role in that business. Techniques like active listening, where you ask questions of the speaker relative to his or her topic, are good if the discussion falters, but my·own experience is that when you give a successful businessperson an opportunity to talk, he or she will. And listening well can create opportunities for you in the near future.

Probably you are thinking, "Of course I listen." I'm sure you do. But I'll bet that as soon as the client points out a problem area in the business, you rush to solution and might even say, "Why, I've had a client before with exactly the same problem and . . ." No!! *One size does not fit all!* And even if it did, no potential client wants to feel his or her experience is not unique. So despite your desire to appear omniscient, experienced, and valuable, hold off that urge to solve the problem as stated and continue to *listen.*

What does this person really mean? Do you understand the terminology being used? If not, do you interrupt to ask for a term definition—and possibly look ignorant in the process since if you really knew the business, you'd know its jargon as well? I haven't found asking someone to define terms has been at all harmful. Banking, the navy, construction—actually every client I've ever had has had special meanings to special terms, and I had to learn them at some point, and from the client.

Do you take notes or merely chat informally? That's a matter of personal preference, as long as it is not disruptive. I make notes of specifics during any meeting, formal or informal, because I can recreate facts more readily later. However, I usually ask the other person if he or she minds if I make a few notes while we talk. No one has ever said no. I've known other consultants who rarely take notes during meetings but jot down important information after the meeting is over while it is still fresh in their minds. The meeting should not be paced according to your stenographic skills, however.

How do *you* act when you meet a prospective client for the first time? Who interviews whom? How do you evaluate whether you can help the prospective client and whether he or she will allow you to do so? Getting answers to the following questions in sequence has worked for me during that initial—and fateful—interview:

1. "What is your business, your role in it, and your view of it?"
2. "What's the problem? You wouldn't have made time for me if you didn't perceive a problem."
3. "I'll rephrase your problem statement. . . . Have I done so correctly? If not, can you expand or correct it?"
4. "How can I help you? Let me describe some areas in which I think we can help you solve your problem."
5. "How do I know I can help you? Let me describe our background relevant to your problems."

The goal of the initial interview is to determine the correctness of fit between the client's needs and the consultant's capabilities. Usually the consultant's own capacity to solve the problems can't be recognized until the client has been able to air his or her own concerns. This five-step sequence has certainly resulted in increased assignments for me. Maybe it can do so for you.

## QUALIFYING PROSPECTIVE CLIENTS: DO THEY REALLY MEAN BUSINESS?

Your initial meeting was to introduce yourselves. If there's nothing there for both of you, then the process should end. You are qualifying one another, and just as the answer to every question is not always yes, the outcome of every introduction is not always an assignment. Remember, you are qualifying, not fantasizing.

You may have to come back another time or more before you or the prospects get to that point where a proposal is asked for. As noted in Chapter 2, your goal should be to put time and effort into a proposal *only* when it has a high likelihood of being accepted, which means you need to ensure that you are not tilting at windmills.

There are some dead giveaways, some negative signs, that this is not a qualified prospect—at least not yet—along with strategies for dealing with them.

## "My Partner Doesn't Realize There's a Problem"

Commonly you'll hear this when a dissenting person in the organization is trying to get others at the same level to deal with a problem. Sometimes your prospect is actually correct, but my experience has been that you'll be used as a cudgel for deeper-rooted problems and may not have an opportunity to do more than slave over a defeated proposal.

Having said that, I do point out that you can sometimes successfully propose a small job that involves canvassing the rest of the management before making a final proposal—and in the process perhaps gain wider support and understanding.

## "Just in Case We Need You"

Insecure managers often use this phrase to help minimize future uncertainty. Sometimes a prospect will say this so as not to hurt your feelings (you do seem like such a nice person—how do I say no?). The danger is that you'll be asked to submit a proposal that will take you a great deal of time yet be destined for the circular file from the outset.

Don't commit to write a proposal *unless you have a clearly definable task*. Always write a confirming letter after the initial meeting but avoid a detailed proposal unless the five-step sequence yields positive information. You can also ask if a proposal would even be appropriate at this stage, which gives your prospect the opportunity to delay it until a later date, when it might be less likely to go into the circular file.

## "Not Invented Here"

If you see a low-budget, do-it-ourselves operation, sometimes your proposal will be the template, and you will have made a lovely blueprint for in-house staff to follow—with no fee for your services. Therefore, don't prepare a proposal in such detail that someone else can pick it up and perform the task. Always leave enough ambiguity that your expertise is required. If you feel that the business cannot support the cost of your implementation, then you have every right to ask the prospect to pay for a detailed proposal that his or her own personnel can implement.

## PREPARING A PROPOSAL

A proposal is a request for commitment and should be administered appropriately. I believe *proposalmanship* is a true art. Because assignments differ even within the same specialty, no single proposal suits every case. However, there are some general guidelines that can be followed.

Jack Schroeder, a strategic planning management consultant, writes among the best proposals I've seen. He is frequently hired by clients just for his ability to write winning proposals on a consistent basis. The sidebar (on pages 136–140) provides some excerpts

## SOME LESSONS LEARNED ABOUT PROPOSALS

During the past 17 years in engineering consulting and management consulting, I've managed the preparation of 30 to 40 formal proposals for consulting services. For the most part, these have been submitted to public agencies, some for my own firm and some for client firms. Potential fees per assignment have ranged from $50,000 to more than $3 million. The success rate has been near 60%, which I attribute to well-balanced overall marketing programs, of which proposals are but one part.

Here are some lessons learned in preparing those proposals:

- A proposal should usually be submitted only when one has some competitive advantage and knows that the chances of being selected for an assignment are good. While there are exceptions, submitting a proposal without some "pre-selling" is usually not effective marketing.

- Proposals may be *solicited* or *unsolicited*. A *solicited* proposal means that the client recognizes that he has a problem and is somewhat committed to devoting resources to a solution. Usually, he already has some fairly well developed idea what the solution is and is looking for someone to carry it out. This is often a highly competitive situation. An *unsolicited* proposal is an opportunity to avoid direct competition and to bring an innovative approach to a problem or project, but is not without risks. The consultant, as an outsider, may misread the situation and propose an inappropriate approach, or may misjudge the willingness of the client to spend money. It's possible, too, that the client will take a good idea and have someone else implement it.

*Source:* F. J. Schroeder, *Some Lessons Learned About Proposals*, West Los Angeles, CA.

- While proposals are nearly always written, that need not be the only way to present qualifications to a potential client. Some firms which provide services which can be visually represented are supplementing their written proposals with videotaped proposals. An audio cassette proposal may have particular potential to reach a busy executive who doesn't have time to read a lengthy written document. For some types of services, a proposal on a computer diskette may be an imaginative way to get the attention of some clients.

- A good proposal, by itself, usually won't get one an assignment, but a bad proposal may lose one an assignment regardless of how closely the qualifications match the assignment need or how much pre-selling has been done. No client wants to be embarrassed by a bad proposal from a consultant he's been championing, or to feel that he's been taken for granted.

- Having weighed the chances of success and having decided to submit a proposal, one should make it a 100% effort. A halfhearted effort will only waste money.

- Managing the proposal preparation effort is a project in itself. Activities necessary to prepare the proposal have to be identified and assigned to responsible parties; resource requirements (e.g., technical writing, word processing, graphics, printing, binding, etc.) have to be identified; and work has to be planned, scheduled and controlled.

- In determining proposal content and organization, clients will want to know exactly the same things we'd all want to know if we were in their place and had to select a consultant:

    How well does the consultant understand the problem or project?

    Specifically, how does the consultant plan to address the project or solve the problem?

How long will it take? What will be the sequence of activities and events?

Who will the consultant use to work on the problem or project? At what stages? On what activities? For how long? What are the credentials of the proposed staff? Have they worked on the same or similar projects elsewhere?

Can the client be assured that the problem will be solved or the assignment carried out successfully under all circumstances? Can the consultant establish, through descriptions of related past work and through client references, that he knows what he's doing?

Why should this consultant clearly be selected above all others? What can be given the client to use in justifying the selection decision to any detractors? (i.e., Can you overcome the "no one ever got fired for selecting IBM" mindset?)

What is the likely cost of the consulting services? Specifically, what is included in and what is excluded from the likely cost?

- Answers to all of these questions will point to the content and organization of the proposal. There will be cases, however, where the manner in which the client has organized his request for a proposal will dictate the manner in which the proposal is organized. Respond in a way which is understandable to the client.

- A well organized proposal will convey that the consultant clearly understands the project or problem, and will address it in a clear, well organized and efficient manner. A vague proposal may convey that the consultant does not clearly understand the problem or its solution. In marketing intangible services, it's essential to move from the vague to the specific. (See the sample Contents page provided on page 140.)

- More and more, clients are interested in directness and brevity. Fortunately, the number of instances where proposals are evaluated by weight seems to be diminishing.

- Usually more can be conveyed with graphics and illustrations than with text. New software makes it easier to make proposals clearer, more interesting and more attractive. Desktop publishing software is being used increasingly to improve the appearance and readability of proposals.

- The form of cost proposals will usually be dictated by the client and the nature of the contract. For lump sum contracts, often no cost detail is required. For hourly, daily or monthly rate contracts with reimbursement of expenses, the client will usually want to see:
  Time for each staff member proposed, unit rates, and extension.
  A complete breakdown of estimated direct expenses, including travel and transportation, per diems, consumable supplies, rental or hourly charges for equipment, etc.
  Overhead and profit, where the breakdown is applicable.
  A total estimated cost for the assignment or project.
  Specific identification of any items of costs which the client may likely incur, but which are not included in the proposal price.

- The proposal should usually also contain the proposed form of contract between the client and consultant. If contract terms have been dictated by the client, have them carefully reviewed by an attorney.

- The marketing effort doesn't stop after the proposal has been submitted. One should follow up with calls to be sure the proposal has been received, to see if more information is needed. Additionally, one should periodically check on the progress of proposal evaluation and reaffirm interest in the assignment.

Finally, one shouldn't give up on a client, even if not selected for an assignment. It's a fact that some clients test a consultant's interest by rejecting the first proposal submitted. Let the client know of interest in future assignments. Often, communicating will be easier once the client knows who the consultant is and what he (or she or they) offers.

## REPRESENTATIVE CONTENTS PAGE
## FOR A MAJOR PROPOSAL

LETTER OF TRANSMITTAL

EXECUTIVE SUMMARY

PROJECT (OR ASSIGNMENT) OVERVIEW
  Introduction
  Understanding of Project (or Assignment) Goals and Issues
  Comments on Client's Scope of Work
  Basis of Proposal

PROJECT (OR ASSIGNMENT) APPROACH AND WORK PLAN
  Location of Work
  Timing of Work
  Description of Consultant's Activities
  Description of Activities by Client and Others
  Project (or Assignment) Reports and Deliverables

PROJECT (OR ASSIGNMENT) ORGANIZATION AND STAFFING
  Organization of the Project Staff
  Curricula Vitae of Proposed Staff Members

QUALIFICATIONS OF CONSULTING FIRM
  Background and Organization of the Firm
  Related Project (or Assignment) Experience
  Client References

COST PROPOSAL (often a separate document)
  Estimated Cost of the Proposed Services
  Costs Not Included in the Proposal

APPENDIXES
  Form of Proposed Agreement or Contract
  Checklist of Information to Be Furnished by the Client
  Representative Final Report Contents

### REPRESENTATIVE LIST OF FIGURES

SCHEMATIC APPROACH

ACTIVITY SCHEDULE

ORGANIZATION CHART

ACTIVITY ASSIGNMENTS

STAFFING SCHEDULE

from his many presentations on proposal writing. Note that even Jack does not capture 100 percent of the assignments on which he proposes—his success rate has been near 60 percent—so try not to set unrealistic goals for yourself as you write your proposals. You can increase your success rate by writing proposals only when you have already prequalified the client and believe you have a *reasonable* chance of winning the assignment.

The following sections cover some points on proposals that *I've* learned the hard way.

## Set a Time Limit

Especially if you are working with the public sector, but even in the private sector, today's hot project can be shelved until funding is secured or other emergencies have settled down. With inflation and other costs varying, you probably would not want to have next year's job quoted at this year's prices, especially as you progress in your consulting career and raise your fees. I always specify the term for which the quoted prices are in effect—usually ninety days but sometimes as short as thirty days.

## Charge for the Proposal

If you feel the prospect may want to do all or part of the work without you or if in order to perform a satisfactory assignment the amount of time you must spend within the company canvassing critical people or resources is high, you are entitled to payment—provided the prospect agrees to such an arrangement. I charge for the visit and then deduct it from any carry-on work that derives from the proposal effort. Sometimes this is the same as dividing the task into phases and merely charging for the requirements gathering that the client would have to pay for under normal circumstances anyhow.

## Limit Your Exposure

If you have to travel far or incur heavy expenses to prepare a proper proposal, you can ask the prospect to defray these expenses. It's a good measure of his or her sincerity too. I know many consultants who will not travel extensively or expensively without such a commitment from the prospect, which automatically winnows out the uninterested suspects.

## Bid Selectively

While you will get better with each proposal you prepare, you will also probably get depressed with each proposal that you lose. At some point you might be the best proposal writer without any assignments. I suggest trying to get as much information as you possibly can on who else is being invited to bid on the opportunity. I know one consultant who always asked what the prospect felt the capture odds were—an interesting question that often displayed how the prospect viewed the project within the company's strategic importance.

## Recycle Proposals

I mean not merely placing the unused copies in your paper recycling bin but formatting your proposals so that they can be excerpted for future opportunities. See Jack's proposed outline format, in the sidebar. You can utilize a boilerplate for much of each proposal, and if you get in the habit of writing up a brief description of each assignment you perform *just after you perform it*, you will soon have a body of cases from which to select those most appropriate for any specific proposal. Exhibit 6-1 provides a sample project write-up.

**Exhibit 6-1**

SAMPLE PROJECT WRITE-UP

---

In a five-year project, Marsha D. Lewin Associates, Inc., provided computer-related support to the prime contractor responsible for the design support for the U.S. Navy reactivation/modernization of the battleships *Missouri* and *Wisconsin*. At all times, meeting tight delivery schedules was vital since the subsystems had to be ready at the appropriate production milestones in the ship repair cycle.

In its entirety, the data processing system controlled, monitored, and reported, for each ship, the repair of 2,000 physical spaces, thousands of drawings and change orders, the progress of thousands of on-site workers, and the information needs of hundreds of managers, including the highest levels of the U.S. Navy. The work was conducted nationwide, with the development of nationwide computer networks to tie in all parties to these massive efforts.

The contributions of Marsha D. Lewin Associates were:

- Requirements analysis, hardware specification and acquisition.

- Selection, customization, and implementation of software to serve the varied needs of over a dozen departments.

- Coordination of multiple operating systems and classes of users.

- Establishment of a hierarchical management information retrieval system according to the requirements of the Naval Sea Systems Command.

- Establishment of a nationwide network of microcomputers and corresponding software.

**Exhibit 6-1**
CONTINUED

- Selection and training of new and in-house data entry and programming personnel to be self-sufficient.

- Architectural design of the software and hardware system.

- Establishment of operational controls and procedures.

Through the efforts of Marsha D. Lewin Associates, Inc. and the prime contractor and subcontractors of this team effort, the *Missouri* and *Wisconsin* project milestones were achieved consistently ahead of schedule and within budget.

Most important, the initial data system plan was designed to be both comprehensive and flexible in meeting new user demands over time. In fact, contractor and civil service personnel were able to quickly maintain the system on their own, and the system proved flexible enough to satisfy a wide variety of new requirements that arose over the life of the program.

# Package Your Assignment to Enable Future Assignments

Often you can propose the assignment to include one or more follow-up visits, wherein you audit the client against preestablished criteria. In case of noncompliance, you might also generate yourself some additional work to rectify the situations you discover.

# COMING TO CLOSURE

Why is it that we consultants typically have such a hard time asking for the sale? The lips tremble, the body shakes, and we avoid the denigrating task. Yet if we don't ask, we are probably reducing our chances of making the sale, so it is absolutely appropriate and professional to ask the prospect when he or she is going to make the decision, whether there is anything else he or she needs to help our chances of success, and if we didn't win this assignment, what the reasons were for our not winning it—and why someone else was selected. At the very least, we can learn from past mistakes and correct them in future proposals.

Sometimes with public agencies, the initial proposal is their way of getting to know you and your organization. Your chances of successfully bidding increase with each proposal as they get to know you better. It is important that you know this about the organization with which you are dealing and are willing to serve your proposal apprenticeship. So in addition to writing the proposal, you should indicate your desire to work for the client and express how important this assignment is to you.

# SIGNING ON THE DOTTED LINE

A contract is not only a good thing to have but, in today's litigious environment, an increasingly important piece of paper. You can include the letter of agreement in your proposal, with an indication that the client need only sign the last page of the letter in the space provided and return to you with the first retainer (if proposed) to start work immediately. Exhibit 2-5 in Chapter 2 shows a sample letter of agreement. You can also have a separate contract, hopefully preapproved by your lawyer as cautioned in early sections. Just to summarize, your contract should cover the following elements:

1. *Payment and billing terms:* How frequently and how much you will be paid. In slower economic times, payments tend to get delayed, so you may want to indicate an interest charge on payments delayed over thirty days. Be sure to indicate the payment terms on each invoice (we write "Payment due net 30").

2. *Scope of work:* Be very careful as to what you promise to do for the client. If you are too broad, you may find yourself responsible for years of follow-up work at no extra fee.

3. *Duration:* Some projects may find themselves subject to delay. If you have additional people on the project and are paying them when such a delay comes in the middle of an assignment, you may find you are subject to increased costs, and without any way of recouping them. I remember one such situation with a client who was consulting to a public agency that had an unforeseen delay in the midst of the project, nearly bankrupting that company as fees were suspended and costs continued.

4. *Guarantees:* If you are performing a productivity improvement assignment, be careful that you do not unwittingly guarantee such increases. You should guarantee only those elements over which you know you have control. For example, if you are writing a software program for a client, be sure to qualify any guarantees with the caveat that it runs only under a specific operating system environment.

5. *Time in force:* To everything there is a season. Especially when you are entering into a time and materials contract, be sure to indicate for how long the contract applies. If you

find that the number of hours anticipated is not needed, you may have an opportunity to use the additional time allocated, provided it is used by a certain date.

6. *Ownership:* If you develop materials in conjunction with the assignment, specify whose property they become. Just in case you've developed the best training materials or the sharpest programs since sliced bread, you should clarify ownership in your client contract to avoid protracted and awkward negotiations (perish the thought of lawsuits) subsequently. I typically leave the ownership to the client anyhow, since I am selling a service, not a product.

7. *Nondisclosure:* With the increasing technology component in most assignments, nondisclosure of technology is very important. So is nondisclosure of client-proprietary information. A clause or two should specify nondisclosure of both parties' strategies and other proprietary data. See Exhibit 3-7 for a sample confidentiality agreement and Exhibit 3-8 for a sample technical nondisclosure agreement.

8. *Arbitration:* Increasingly disputes are being settled through arbitration rather than in the courts. Such specification in the contract, provided both parties agree to it, can reduce costs of subsequent litigation materially and reduce delays in finally getting the issues resolved in the court system. However, the goal is to avoid legal battles between you and your clients if at all possible.

9. *Parties:* Some public sector clients demand that the proposal identify by name personnel to be used on the assignment, with any changes in those assignments made only with the client's specific and written approval. Determine if the personnel must be specified in the contract, and, if so, be sure to include within the contract the mechanism for changing those so named.

# PERFORMING THE WORK

The whole purpose of selling is to give you the opportunity to perform your magic: consulting in your specialty for your new client. As you conduct your assignment, there are a few words of caution to add.

## Watch Your Back

Often a consultant is perceived by the company's employees (and even some management) as a hired hand from the outside whose efforts will reduce their numbers, their scope, or their power. Sometimes these feelings can result in outright hostility (which can be tolerated) or downright sabotage (which is harder to work through). Stay alert to such possibilities, and be sure that you have covered such eventualities through your contract. Avoid adding any fuel to existing fires through your own actions on the job.

You are essentially coming in as the new kid on the block—and the corporate bully may try to test your mettle to see just how good you really are.

## Avoid Taking Sides

Sometimes you *must* take sides as part of your assignment, but be sure to avoid doing so unnecessarily. Remember that you were brought in from the outside because you are supposed to be *more objective* than internal folks would be. And, as a corollary, try to minimize displays of favoritism. All of us encounter individuals we clearly prefer over others, but expressing such favoritism inappropriately can reduce that person's effectiveness within the organization if his or her ascendancy or praise is seen as due to an outsider's perception, not internally ordained.

## Remember: You're Not Family

A common mistake I observe (in myself as well as others, especially when we have been working with a client for an extended period) is that we forget that we are even more removed than in-laws and we are not family. We are, above all, outsiders who can leave the environment, which always is empowering for us. As such, we do not necessarily have the same stake in what is transpiring as the employees who will be staying there long after we're gone.

Two aspects of this issue are that we cannot say and do what employees can say or do without having a different impact, and, more important, we must be sure to leave a legacy for the company that can sustain it. For example, if I indicate that a computer operator is not knowledgeable of certain software products, I always add that *it would not be expected for him or her to have that knowledge without specific training*—because the client imputes to me that I am talking as the expert. Without adding the qualifying clause, it could be interpreted that he *should* have that knowledge. Or if a computer operator is put into a "suicide job"—where the task is clearly too big for a single individual to handle over time—I must be sure to specify in the organizational description that such a situation will develop in the future, lest they perceive the operator as not being capable of handling the task. After all, the task has changed, and could be foreseen to do so.

## Remain Objective

If you feel you cannot do so, get out, for all of the reasons already noted. Performing the technical aspects of our assignments in many ways remains the easiest part of consulting; it's managing the politics of any assignment that presents the challenge. You are generally managing multiple constituencies, and your ultimate success as a consultant depends on your doing that well.

## Do Good Work

Indeed this is the most important of all. Your continued success depends on your performing each assignment for each client as if it were the most important assignment of your career—because it *is*! And since this is the section on selling, if you do good work, you have a built-in opportunity to continue to generate new work for your client, who is satisfied. Now that you are familiar with the company, you are more valuable for working on future assignments.

## SELLING TO A CLIENT

Many good assignments can be had from an existing or previous client, much to your advantage: You are already known and proven to your client and familiar with the company and the way in which it transacts business. You also are reasonably familiar with the cast of characters upon which your next proposal must be based. That knowledge allows you to estimate more clearly what it will cost your client for you to do a subsequent job.

Whether you charge for a proposal for new work should be dealt with on a case-by-case basis, but the rule of thumb I use is that I do not charge for a proposal if I initiate it; if the client asks me to generate a proposal (to show to someone else within the organization, for example) I will ask if that's to be for fee before I write the proposal. If not, then I can make the decision as to whether I feel I want to spend the time on doing so (I usually do).

If you are doing additional work under the same contract, be sure that you do not embark upon territory not covered by your existing contract. I once was in the midst of a job as a sole proprietorship when I became incorporated again. Although action was required to be taken at the board of supervisors level, I did so to ensure that the contracts were modified to cover Marsha D. Lewin Associates, *Inc.* Otherwise I would not have been able to have the coverage afforded by incorporation because of the prior contract wording.

## SELLING IN THE AFTERGLOW

We often forget that the easiest market to sell to is our previous clients. However, far too frequently we end up involved in lengthy client assignments and forget to come up for air enough to maintain our relationships with *previous* clients. This is especially true when we have clients in disparate geographic regions. You can't drop in for a luncheon engagement in Phoenix when you're almost full time in Dallas.

Keeping in touch after completion of the assignment is a definite challenge but not an impossible one. I use techniques similar to those I use with prospects: sending articles that might be of interest, sending Christmas cards or an occasional note, telephone call, an attempt to lunch or breakfast or drop by if convenient. Keeping in touch with your satisfied clients, as we hope each one will be, has many benefits. I've obtained additional assignments by this method; I maintain a pool of clients who are available for references and happily provide them, and I continue to receive information on the marketplace—who is doing what to whom not only in the company but in the industry in general.

## WHAT TO BILL FOR

When billing your clients, include those items for which you will be paid that are covered within the contract. However, there are those occasional judgment calls. I generally exclude from billing on time and materials assignments any time spent on mistakes of my own causing and any time due to learning that is not explicitly covered by the contractual terms. The general rule of thumb is that if it is not directly required by my existing assignment, I don't charge for the time spent on it. If it becomes of value in a future assignment, then I've wisely invested my time in developing a marketable skill or contact.

# CHAPTER 7

# Leveraging Yourself

Unless you are one of the fortunate few who is able to clone himself or herself or find a yang for your yin that complements you utterly, you will be destined to manage your practice yourself for the foreseeable future. And that becomes the dilemma of the entre- preneurial consultant: minimizing the swings in the characteristic work–seek work cycle. One of the ways in which you can do so is to leverage yourself by selling additional services or products or to sell the services of others.

## WHEN CAN YOU OFFER MORE TO YOUR CLIENTS?

Before you start thinking of adding brushes to your sales product line, let's establish some guidelines for what makes sense for you to sell. The purpose of leveraging yourself is to make it easier for people to reach you, which I believe comes from their ability to identify you and what you can do for them more clearly. If you offer too wide or diverse a range of services, you can send a mixed message to your marketplace that makes it *harder* rather than easier for you to market yourself.

I have known far too many consultants who are more entrepreneurial than *consultant.* They sell computer hardware and software; they sell discounted long-distance telephone services; they sell whatever appears to offer an opportunity to make some money. Not only are there dangers of running into conflicts of interest by doing so (just which computer vendor's hardware do you recommend when you represent one or more vendors?), and compromising any claims you may make as to your objectivity as a consultant, but if the vendor falls into disfavor, you may lose your marketing edge and the opportunity you thought you had to make that additional money. I've been approached by many vendors over the course of my consulting career but for those reasons always back off from their offers to sell their products. I believe that I've made more money as a result of that independent stance.

I often see consultants who try to leverage themselves by proffering themselves in this week's specialty buzzword—business process reengineering, total quality, downsizing—all of which makes it harder for me to pigeonhole their services into something I'll recollect quickly when I'm seeking to refer another consultant. In fact, such creeping expertise works against such consultants, as I tend to pigeonhole them—into the specialists who are nonrecommendable: jack of all trades but master of none. So if you decide to leverage yourself by adding more services to your existing base, which is an especially good strategy in cyclical businesses such as ours, do it in *related* areas. For example, interim information system division management is closely allied with information technology consulting. The addition of the interim management function does not detract from the basic specialty because it is still associated with information technology, which would not be the case if only "interim management" appeared on the consultant's business card. Further, if you are trying to evolve or sustain a high-tech image, going into areas or selling products that do not reinforce that image would hurt you—for example, selling an automated personnel evaluation product when you market yourself as a people-oriented personnel consultant.

## SELLING WHAT YOU KNOW

You can "productize" yourself appropriately by selling books, audiotapes, videotapes, and other materials that are right in line with what you do. For example, Mickey Rosenau has written a number of excellent books on project management and new product development, his areas of expertise. Additionally, he has taught a number of fine seminars and sold case studies so that others can buy them to use in seminars.

The secret to selling such materials is that they should be related to your consulting specialty and enhance your reputation; otherwise they merely contribute even further to your fragmented image. I have audiotapes, some videotapes, and a book on software project management I coauthored with Mickey. I cannot trace clients directly to any of them, but they do strengthen my reputation as an expert in information technology and its management. When I meet with clients, they are more impressed than without them.

Have I made money from these adjunct projects? Some, but certainly not enough to retire on or to sustain me. However, they have helped indirectly to keep my name in front of the public and to establish credibility. And once the major work was accomplished, there was little else to do. I even self-published the book when the publisher sold out the first edition and continue to make modest sales annually—without having to do anything other than fill the orders. However, I did not have to invest any of my money to create the audiotapes and videotapes.

I have heard countless consultants tell tales of woe about investing in audiotapes and videotapes, spending more time and money than they ever were able to make in sales. Again, as with marketing your consulting services, marketing a product needs a distribution channel. You will have to share in the product sales with a distributor (if you can find one willing to take your product on), and you lay out the costs for developing the package up front.

If you do not express yourself well on paper, then books (and articles as well) may not be the best medium for you. And if you experience paralyzing camera fear, videos may not be the best vehicle either. As with any of these adjunct products, competence is what you should be able to demonstrate so that they work *for* you, not against you.

## SELLING OTHER CONSULTANTS' SERVICES

There are two varieties of selling others: where you bill for them and where you receive an initial finder's fee, and then the consultant bills the client directly. The advantages of the former are that you know exactly how much the client is paying and can take the correct percentage from the fees. The disadvantage is the bookkeeping involved on a continuing basis. The advantage of the latter is that you make a placement and then get your monies up front. Arrangements for follow-on work derived from the basic contract can be hard to control, of course.

I know consultants who have made money by selling other consultants and taking a finder's fee. I have strong feelings against doing so, because then I believe you're acting as an agent, not as a consultant. Although we have had assignments where many other consultants have been involved, they have been under our banner, and my organization has assumed liability and responsibility for the work performed. In fact, when we've had opportunities to perform work that did not contribute to our overall strategic direction or was too small to warrant the administrative overhead required when we take on a new client, I've referred the task directly to one of our reliable subcontractors, who handled the assignment alone.

I think you sell differently when someone else is responsible for performing the task, and I do not want to be in the "body shop" business, or contract programming, as it is called in my specialty. However, it has been lucrative for many other people. Whether this is truly consulting is open to much speculation. It is most definitely entrepreneurial, however.

Do you tell the client when a finder's fee is involved? I believe you should, because a referral without fee could be perceived very differently by the client from one where you are getting a fee for doing so. The passing of money *could* affect your objectivity. Who is responsible for telling the client of the fee? The referring consultant, who is dealing with the client and choreographing the situation. It might well compromise the client's relationship with the referring consultant if it were to come out later.

## SUMMARY

You can leverage yourself by selling other services, products, and people, but you risk diluting your focus as a consultant.

# CHAPTER 8

# Using the Computer Effectively

**I** truly cannot see how an entrepreneurial consultant can maintain an effective practice without a computer. The personal computer has hastened the demise of the office secretarial pool—which is just as well for solo consultants, who don't have access to one anyhow. Computer software readily available to the public is also applicable for keeping financial records, mailing lists, and databases of client information. The computer has become the office factotum and best assistant any entrepreneurial consultant could have.

I do not recommend any specific software products, because as soon as such recommendations are made, they are outdated by newer developments in the field. However, I do point out generic products that should be part of any technically savvy consultant's techno-office.

# FULL OF SOUND AND FURY: SETTING UP YOUR SYSTEM

Once upon a time—what seems like eons ago—a computer was best used for keeping accounting records. Today's computers can do more than mainframe expatriates ever envisioned. Your system should, at a minimum, consist of:

- A high-quality color monitor (super VGA).
- The maximum amount of memory (RAM) you can afford.
- The fastest chip you can afford (Pentium, 586).
- A keyboard.
- Fax modem capability (minimum 14,400 baud speed).
- The largest available hard disk drive (at least 250 megabytes).
- At least one floppy drive: high-density 3½ inches (but if you have clients with older systems you might want to have a second drive with a 5¼-inch high-density drive).
- A tape cartridge backup (120 megabyte capacity requires more than two tapes to back up).
- The best-quality laser printer you can afford (Hewlett-Packard is the industry standard).

The following optional items are becoming standard:

- CD-ROM (for dictionaries, reference books, loading large-sized software).
- Speakers and microphone.
- Scanner.

You will need as well the associated cables, boards, and software drivers. (Like being chauffeured around, these wonderful devices need to be "driven" around your system.)

For software, the operating system should have a graphical user interface such as Microsoft's Windows and you should budget for the following specific product categories:

- Word processor.
- Spreadsheet, with graphics capability.
- Accounting program.
- Calendar and organizer.
- Mailing list and database programs.
- Communications software to an online service such as Compu-Serve, America On-Line, and/or the Internet.
- Presentation developer.
- Virus detection software (especially if you transfer files among machines).

Optional software includes the following items:

- Charting software (to create graphic representations of organization charts, data flows, etc.).
- Project management software.
- Special templates for any standard programs.
- Special fonts and clip art.

The electronic office is *here* to stay, and you can lose yourself in the technology if you give yourself half an opportunity. Before you go off the deep end, ask yourself how many different fonts you actually use in a standard letter. Which fonts do you continually use, to enable a standard image of your business to emerge?

Much of the rest of this chapter describes some practical applications that your computer can generate.

## SETTING UP A FILE INDEX

As mentioned in Chapter 3, my filing system keeps me organized. After I've reviewed the files, I archive them. Often I need to refer back to them. In the early days (and some later days too) I would look at the file folder list typed up and taped to the outside of each storage box. Then I'd dig through the box for the needed folder. After moves and earthquakes, those lists were ripped, and a new method was implemented. Now as a box is filled, its contents are entered into a spreadsheet, and when I want to find a particular topic, I merely search for the particular file name in my spreadsheet and know immediately which box to go to. A sample of the spreadsheet is shown in Exhibit 8-1.

## GENERATING CLIENT INVOICES

A template in my spreadsheet program automatically computes the net amount due for each invoice, as shown in Exhibit 8-2. The italicized items are entered for each invoice; the nonitalicized items are then calculated automatically by the software.

## MAINTAINING A MAILING LIST

We've amassed a list for mailing to clients, contacts, peers, and others during the past twenty-five years. Our original mailing list was created in a now-defunct software product. Although the product itself was still serviceable, making changes to the software became difficult, and my needs continued to evolve, so I needed flexibility. We switched the mailing list to a spreadsheet, which can be imported into a word processor to create mailing labels or envelopes and it can be searched through when I wish to find addresses or telephone numbers of specific people or the names of contacts in a specific state (for example, when I travel back to New York City). The spreadsheet features the following:

- Title (e.g., Dr., Prof., Mr., Mrs.).
- First name.
- Middle initial.
- Last name.
- Position.
- Company name.
- Address.
- City.
- State and zip code.
- Telephone and fax numbers.
- Date the information was entered in the data base.
- A code for each entry, to reflect the person's origin and interests (e.g., business, client, professional association and which).

# COMPUTING PROJECT PROFITABILITY

On some projects, a large number of subcontractors work for us, and the computation of these invoices for subsequent payment can be extremely time-consuming. I have two spreadsheets. One, computed for each invoice, which verifies the calculations on each invoice submitted, calculates a single subtotal for each expense category for submission to the client, and calculates the net amount due in fees to the subcontractors. Exhibit 8-3 shows an example. A second spreadsheet is a cumulative total of the labor costs incurred from all subcontractor invoices submitted to date. The amount remaining in each work order is also calculated. Exhibit 8-4 is an example of this spreadsheet. Both spreadsheets are easy to maintain, and efficiently reconcile, calculate, and record information in a manageable form.

**Exhibit 8-1**

BOX INVENTORY SHEET

| BOX # | FOLDER TITLE | COMPANY | DETAIL | COMMENTS | COLOR | MISC. |
|---|---|---|---|---|---|---|
| 21 | transaction logs | mdla | sole proprietorship | 1992 | pink | |
| 21 | trial balance | mdla | | 1992 | pink | |
| 21 | business taxes | mdla | | 1992 | pink | |
| 21 | bank statements | mdla | City National Bank | 1993 | purple | |
| 21 | trial balance | mdla | | 1993 | purple | |
| 21 | income statement | mdla | | 1993 | purple | |
| 21 | transaction logs | mdla | | 1993 | purple | |
| 21 | business records | mdla | | 1993 | purple | |
| 21 | business receipts | mdla | | 1993 | purple | |
| 11 | Smith Properties | Smith | | — | blue | |
| 11 | Schweid Company | Schweid | contract | 1992 | orange | |

**Exhibit 8-2**

SAMPLE INVOICE

---

17-Dec-95

Mr. Client Company President
Client Company
2 Park Plaza, Suite 10
Los Angeles, CA 90019

| RE: | Consultant Services Rendered | | |
|---|---|---|---|
| | Client Assignment | | |
| | Phase I | | |
| | Purchase Order Number: | 7634 | |
| | MDLA Invoice No: | 95-002 | |

Fees:

| | semi-monthly billing | month #1 | $20,000.00 |
|---|---|---|---|

Expenses:

| | 95 miles @ $0.290 | $27.55 | |
|---|---|---|---|
| | telephone | $ 0.00 | |
| | subsistence | $ 0.00 | |
| | repro/fedex | $ 0.00 | |
| | parking | $ 0.00 | |
| | other | $ 0.00 | |
| | Total Expenses: | | $    27.55 |

TOTAL DUE THIS INVOICE:                    $20,027.55

Payment terms: net 30 from invoice date
**THANK YOU**

---

**Exhibit 8-3**

SAMPLE BILLING WORKSHEET, SHOWING TYPE OF EXPENSE PER STAFF MEMBER

| A | B | C | D | E | F | G | H | I | J | K | L | M |
|---|---|---|---|---|---|---|---|---|---|---|---|---|
| 1 | | | | | | | | | | | | |
| 2 | | | | | For Billing Ending | | 17-Jan-96 | | | | | |
| 3 | | | | | | | | | | | | |
| 4 | INDIV | PHONE | SUBSIST | REPRO | FEDEX | MILEAGE | MILEAGE $ | PARKING | OTHER | TOTAL | FEES | GR TOT |
| 5 | MARY | $30.00 | $82.69 | $81.53 | $13.00 | 1135 | $329.15 | $0.00 | $0.00 | $536.37 | | $536.37 |
| 6 | LOIS | $0.00 | $0.00 | $0.00 | $0.00 | 0 | $0.00 | $0.00 | $0.00 | $0.00 | | $0.00 |
| 7 | HENRI | | | $0.00 | | 0 | $0.00 | | | $0.00 | $700.00 | $700.00 |
| 8 | PHIL | $0.00 | $0.00 | $0.00 | | 0 | $0.00 | $0.00 | $0.00 | $0.00 | $0.00 | $0.00 |
| 9 | JAN | $0.00 | $0.00 | $0.00 | $0.00 | 0 | $0.00 | $0.00 | $0.00 | $0.00 | $0.00 | $0.00 |
| 10 | HOWIE | | | | | 0 | $0.00 | | | $0.00 | $465.25 | $465.25 |
| 11 | MARVIN | $61.69 | | $37.68 | | 605 | $175.45 | $0.00 | $0.00 | $274.82 | $3,612.00 | $3,886.82 |
| 12 | IMRE | | | $0.00 | | 0 | $0.00 | | | | $370.00 | $370.00 |
| 13 | TOTALS: | $91.69 | $82.69 | $119.21 | $13.00 | 1740 | $504.60 | $0.00 | $0.00 | $811.19 | $5,147.25 | $5,958.44 |
| 14 | | | | | | | | | | $0.00 | | $0.00 |

## Exhibit 8-4
### CUMULATIVE BILLINGS SPREADSHEET, FOR ALL STAFF

| | A | B | C | D | E | F | G | H | I | J |
|---|---|---|---|---|---|---|---|---|---|---|
| 1 | | | | | For Billing Ending | 17-Jan-96 | | | | |
| 2 | INDIVIDUAL | MARY | LOIS | HENRI | PHIL | JAN | HOWIE | MARVIN | IMRE | GR TOT |
| 3 | BILL 001 | | | | | | | | $1,680.00 | $1,680.00 |
| 4 | BILL 002 | | | | | $325.00 | | $178.00 | | $503.00 |
| 5 | BILL 003 | | | | $687.50 | $1,025.00 | | $246.25 | $2,604.00 | $4,562.75 |
| 6 | BILL 004 | | | | $425.00 | $1,700.00 | | | $4,053.00 | $6,178.00 |
| 7 | BILL 005 | | | | $400.00 | $625.00 | | $535.25 | $3,150.00 | $4,710.25 |
| 8 | BILL 006 | | | $10,336.00 | $700.00 | | $1,331.25 | $465.25 | $3,612.00 | $16,444.50 |
| 9 | BILL 007 | | $300.00 | | | $887.50 | $712.50 | $550.75 | $4,074.00 | $6,824.75 |
| 10 | TOTAL | $300.00 | $300.00 | $10,336.00 | $2,212.50 | $4,562.50 | $2,043.75 | $1,975.50 | $19,173.00 | $40,903.25 |
| 11 | WORK ORDER | $500.00 | $300.00 | $10,000.00 | $2,500.00 | $6,000.00 | $2,800.00 | $2,500.00 | $25,000.00 | |
| 12 | LEFT IN WO | $200.00 | $0.00 | ($336.00) | $287.50 | $1,437.50 | $756.25 | $524.50 | $5,827.00 | |

# MAINTAINING ACCOUNTING RECORDS

The oldest software package on our machine is a DOS-based accounting package acquired a decade ago that still functions well. It provides standard accounting reports in a timely manner and allows us to cut checks. We can monitor each project, which is set up as a separate account class, as to profitability. Your accountant can help you in selecting or customizing your own accounting system. To share our own experience with you, our reports are:

*Chart of Accounts:* organized into a numerical designation for each project (the last two digits are the same) income and expense class. This allows us to report each project and monitor profitability by project. For example, accounts 30103 and 31003 are the fees and reimbursable expense income accounts. Accounts exist for every expense or income class we need to track, for the company as a whole and for each project. Fewer classes exist for projects, such as subcontractor costs and direct expenses (expense side), and fees and reimbursable expenses paid (income side). Many more classes exist on the company level, such as telephone, marketing, utilities, and supplies in the expense category, and interest income.

*Balance Sheet:* reflects the value or worth of our company. We can compare the current year's balance sheet to the previous year's, which I find helpful for trend analysis. Our asset side is comprised only of our cash and current value of office equipment and furnishings (original value less depreciation). I maintain a separate sheet of pending receivables because we are on a cash accounting basis.

*Income Statement:* also called the P&L (Profit & Loss) statement, is important in monitoring how the company is doing. If expenses exceed income too frequently, the business may well be in trouble. We can compare this month this year to the same month last year, and year to date this year to last year's figures. If your consulting is cyclical, the year to date figures would be more important to you than the monthly figures. Many of the accounts in the chart of accounts are rolled into a single line on this report.

*Project Statement:* shows profit and loss by individual project, in the same format as the income statement for the entire business. This is very helpful in determining how profitable any single assignment is.

*Trial Balance:* shows every transaction by account number for the month. Because ours is a double-entry accounting system, the sum of all debits must be identical with all credits for the company's "ledger" to balance.

*Transaction Log:* as the name implies, is a printed record of all transactions, which are entered. A variety of sequences are available, such as by account or by transaction type (for example, income or expense).

However, what our accounting system does *not* do is display numbers graphically, which is much easier to work with today. Thus, the package's days are numbered, and when inertia is overcome by the need for a glitzier representation, we'll replace the package with one that allows me to retrieve graphic trends.

Not all elderly software needs to be retired and placed on techno-Medicare. However, the cost of adapting some of the older software is now typically more than buying new packages that are Windows based and have full graphics display capabilities. And it's much easier to get support from today's new family of office-support software.

# PREPARING PRESENTATIONS

My new enchantment is my presentation software, which allows me to create an on-screen show or transparencies, handouts, and speakers' notes for any talk. I've used it many times already and find that clients enjoy following the on-screen presentation. I can add sound when I get the necessary speakers for greater effect and will probably do so—when I get some free time. I have the necessary viewing software on my laptop, which I can easily take with me to a client presentation.

There are many different ways of implementing some of the basic consulting practice functions. With today's word processing software, you could, for example, perform with the word processor calculations that formerly were done only in spreadsheets. Perhaps this will serve as an incentive to mobilize your technology to allow you to spend your working hours consulting, not administrating.

# TRAVELING THE INFORMATION SUPERHIGHWAY

Internet has become all the rage of late, but electronic mail, or e-mail, has been around for decades. During the 1980s, online services such as CompuServe became popular; this decade has thus far seen the interconnection of the various online services so that you can communicate with anyone, anywhere, without regard to specific carrier. What does that bode for you? Probably that you'll be able to contact vendors and suppliers electronically, saving countless hours and dollars of telephone time; that you will be able to order your office supplies, invoice your clients, and transmit your bill electronically; that you can work at your optimum times and quickly deliver your results to your clients, without waiting for pickup by

**Exhibit 8-5**

TYPICAL E-MAIL MESSAGE

---

FROM:         Username, 55555,555
TO:           Marsha D. Lewin, 72622,3112
DATE:         1/3/96 3:54 PM

Re:           On-site Use Manual Meeting 1/15/96

I am aware of the changes required in the user manual. I've sent an e-mail update to all recipients of the manual and I believe the subjects are now addressed properly in the document. The next release of the manual will be 1/23/96.

I will be out on 1/15 to deliver two technical bulletins and would like to meet with you at 11:00 in the small conference room at the site. Please let me know if this is not convenient.

---

your overnight carrier. (Even overnight sounds slow by comparison with the concept of an eternally accessible transmission capability!)

A typical e-mail message available through online carriers is shown in Exhibit 8-5. Miraculously, no stamps even need to be licked, and no envelope needs to be sealed. It's a simple sequence of button pressing now.

Years ago, an older consultant enthusiastically described his efficient, state-of-the-art virtual office: files were exchanged through "the sneakernet" provided by his secretary, who drove between the homes of the various consultants working on a particular job, picking up tapes and drafts on disks, finalizing them, and delivering them personally to their destinations or sending them by overnight carrier. Now the goal of the virtual office has truly been attained: I draft a document; upload it to CompuServe, where my associate picks it up, reads it, makes any changes to it, and uploads the revised file again; and then my secretary picks it off, finalizes it, prepares the copies, and disposes of them, sometimes even using CompuServe again, since so many of our clients now have the service. Today's technology has allowed us to assemble consultants who are not physically colocated into a virtual organization to better serve our clients.

A benefit of this arrangement is that it irons out the differences in the biorhythms of my associate and me. He excels at last-minute, late-night creativity. I have lost that capability, and find that my two gray cells refuse to rub together and ignite much of anything when I'm busy rubbing my eyes. The continuous access to information enables the circadian rhythm to occur when it needs to, without requiring one of us to compromise our own scheduling.

*Unless you want to be left behind you'd better get on the information superhighway*—at least onto one of the online services, and *now.* More and more services and products will be bought and sold online, and if you're not part of that marketplace, you'll surely be left behind. Why decrease your marketplace when you can increase it at almost no cost?


## TECHNOMARKETING TIPS

If you decide to use the information superhighway to offer your wares, be sure to keep your descriptions brief, and have files containing your vital data ready to upload at a moment's notice. All of the standard courtesies still apply: If you use someone as a reference in your electronically transmitted materials, be sure to ask permission and also let the person know who might be calling him or her and why. Of course, if your references are also online you can quickly fire off an e-mail message to let them know.

Although you can conduct an assignment entirely through

uploading and downloading, *meeting the client face to face still is the best way to land the assignment.* You could, of course, add your picture, scanned in, to your résumé, so that the recipient has a sense of what you look like, not just how you express yourself on electronic paper.

If you have the presentation software, you could create a presentation, and a recipient with the same software at his or her end could run the file and have a personalized on-screen show to get to know your work even better. The balance to strike is between the assumptions you make about the technology at the receiving end of your file, the number of disks it will take to hold your full-blown offering, and the image you are trying to project.

## FAX AROUND THE CLOCK

I've said before that a fax is indispensable to the efficient consultant. You can fax a document from your computer directly to the recipient; however, unless you leave your computer on continually, receiving faxes is much more cumbersome, requiring you to call the recipient first to have his or her machine turned on when you wish to send. For that reason, I have my old fax machine and will replace it—but with a plain paper fax—when it goes to electronic heaven.

# PART THREE

# Survival Issues in Consulting

## Is This Really How You Want to Spend Your Life?

# CHAPTER 9

# Ethical Consulting

The 1990s have seen ethics come out of the closet and into the boardroom; they are no longer presumed but clearly articulated. Adherence to a code of ethics is now a marketable aspect and admirable business attribute. I've just seen a best friend return to law school to obtain her degree so she can enter the nascent field of medical ethics.

We must know what ethics means to determine if we run our business according to them. Webster defines *ethics* as "the system or code of morals of a particular person, religion, group, profession, etc." and *ethical* as "conforming to the standards of conduct of a given profession or group." The Business Ethics Forum in California defines *ethical* as "evaluation of a particular decision as to whether it satisfies or optimizes value-based criteria regarding right and wrong or good and bad."

In general, businesses must be run according to a predefined set of values that are acceptable—presumably to the clients as well as to consultants. Otherwise we would bend with the exigencies of volatile economies, difficult clients, and crass opportunism. Especially as professionals who operate alone, adherence to a common body of professionally accepted values is important for our clients as well as for our own sense of direction.

The Institute of Management Consultants has its own code of ethics, shown in Exhibit 9-1. Members of the Institute must sign an affirmation of their adherence to this code when they renew their annual membership. The code creates the set of moral expectations that the client can expect from the consultant and that the consultant can expect of himself or herself. The tenets are reasonable yet surprisingly many consultant wanna-bes violate precepts by accepting jobs they're not qualified for, by being loose-lipped and revealing information about clients to others, and most important, by losing the objectivity so important in delivering a consulting service to our client constituency.

A code of ethics requires an enforcement procedure if it is to be effective. Typically, organizations and societies with ethical codes have an evaluation procedure; if the accused fails, the result is expulsion from the society or ostracism. This is true of the Institute of Management Consultants, its predecessor organization—the Association of Management Consultants, and most other professional associations I am familiar with.

As our lives become more complicated, the application of ethics is no longer simply an eye for an eye. For example, we are becoming an international economy, with international consulting assignments. Ethics are culturally dependent; taking *bakshish* (kickbacks) is illegal in the United States, for example, but you cannot do business in the Middle Eastern countries without it. Where on the ethical continuum would you solve that problem? (I do not do business in that part of the world as a prime contractor, although more American companies and agencies are moving in.)

Exhibit 9-1

# CODE OF ETHICS

## Clients

1. We will serve our clients with integrity, competence, and objectivity.

2. We will keep client information and records of client engagements confidential and will use proprietary client information only with the client's permission.

3. We will not take advantage of confidential client information for ourselves or our firms.

4. We will not allow conflicts of interest which provide a competitive advantage to one client through our use of confidential information from another client who is a direct competitor without that competitor's permission.

## Engagements

5. We will accept only engagements for which we are qualified by our experience and competence.

6. We will assign staff to client engagements in accord with their experience, knowledge, and expertise.

7. We will immediately acknowledge any influences on our objectivity to our clients and will offer to withdraw from a consulting engagement when our objectivity or integrity may be impaired.

## Fees

8. We will agree independently and in advance on the basis for our fees and expenses and will charge fees and expenses that are reasonable, legitimate, and commensurate with the services we deliver and the responsibility we accept.

9. We will disclose to our clients in advance any fees or commissions that we will receive for equipment, supplies or services we recommend to our clients.

## Profession

10. We will respect the intellectual property rights of our clients, other consulting firms, and sole practitioners and will not use proprietary information or methodologies without permission.

11. We will not advertise our services in a deceptive manner and will not misrepresent the consulting profession, consulting firms, or sole practitioners.

12. We will report violations of this Code of Ethics.

The Council of Consulting Organizations, Inc. Board of Directors approved this Code of Ethics on January 8, 1991. The Institute of Management Consultants (IMC) is a division of the Council of Consulting Organizations, Inc.

**IMC** INSTITUTE OF MANAGEMENT CONSULTANTS
521 Fifth Avenue, 35th Floor, New York, NY 10175-3598

Printed with permission of the Institute of Management Consultants.

Do you maximize profits in the short term and forfeit the long-term potential of your client's company? An older consulting company was looked down upon for decades because it was reputed to drain the long-term viability of a client company in order to show short-term profits, *on which its fees were based.* Presumably if the fees were not based on the short-term effects, the action would not be as nefarious.

## ETHICS AND YOU

If you find yourself in doubt about an action, you can validate it against the code. If you still cannot resolve it, apply Mickey Rosenau's *"New York Times* rule" which I mentioned in Chapter 2 and restate here: Don't do anything you wouldn't want to read about in the banner headline of tomorrow's *New York Times.* If you still have any ambiguity, err in the direction of omission rather than commission: Don't do something that might be ethically ambiguous. It is far better to be conservative in these issues. As Shakespeare said through Polonius in *Hamlet:* "This above all, to thine own self be true, and it must follow as the night the day, thou canst not then be false to any man."

The ethical basis of consulting boils down to the eternal Golden Rule: *Do unto others as you would have them do unto you.* That means you show to your client respect, discretion, honesty, and appropriateness, as we would have them do to us.

## WHEN TO SAY NO

The areas of illegality are generally clear: Don't commit fraud, cook the books, or steal. But there are gray areas of how we represent the facts—with modulated phrases, for example, to be better received. Is that unethical? If you are being asked to do something illegal, don't do it. You jeopardize your future and compromise yourself. Nothing is worth that. And if you *feel* something is illegal, whether it might be or not to others is not even the issue; you'll compromise yourself because it's illegal in your book, according to your code of ethics. If you are violating the Golden Rule, you should say *No!*

## WHAT YES REALLY MEANS

When we say yes to our clients, we are bound by our commitment to do the very best we can for them during the assignment—and to be as discreet as we can after the assignment has been completed in our references to that client. It is, in that sense, a lifelong relationship we are taking on, not merely a temporary assignment. "Yes" means that we are committed to do more than what the contract calls for—to deliver that 150 percent, not 100 percent—and deliver excellence.

By now, we're all familiar with the phrase "search for excellence." To consultants, excellence means effective delivery of a necessary service to a client who appreciates high quality. Here are some techniques you can use to help achieve that excellence:

**1.** Establish standards, and never compromise yourself in adherence to them. Set them high, and your employees will follow your lead.

**2.** Ensure that the professionalism in the people who work for you lives up to your standards (dress, technical and professional competence, currency of knowledge, attitude, etc.). Your company name and reputation are at stake.

3. Select your clients carefully. Avoid those who don't appreciate your high quality of consulting services. If clients apply pressure for your firm to deliver a product of which you are not going to be proud, it makes you less than excellent.

# CHAPTER 10

---

# Managing Stress

Consultants lead a life that, by all external measures, appears exciting: dashing from one airport terminal to another, sitting cheek by jowl with the leaders of businesses, landing large assignments, phone in one hand and these days a second phone in the other. Stimulating, challenging, and most definitely *fatiguing*. Creeping fatigue seems to make its way into our lives and personalities, as we optimize every moment, trade downtime for just one more temporary professional activity, stay up late just one more night polishing off that proposal, zone out at our son's or daughter's soccer game while we mull over the alternatives of a knotty problem that surfaced at a client's. We can't let go and end up maximizing every waking moment with work-related activities.

## THE PRESSURE COOKER

If you've ever watched a pressure cooker, there is little advanced warning that the proper temperature has been achieved. Suddenly off the pot goes: white smoke wheezing, top shaking, and it takes a while to slow down, even after the heat has been turned off. The analogy is fairly obvious: When we get overloaded, often through the creeping fatigue syndrome, we finally go off, and even after we push ourselves away from the stressors in our lives, we still simmer for a while until we can get back to a less stressed state.

But, you say, we are intelligent, aware individuals, who as practicing professionals continue to calibrate ourselves. We are aware of when we are not taking care of ourselves adequately. That may be true, but every so often we overstep the limits of adequacy and enter the realm of too much. I have always found it difficult to sustain balance in my life. As a project-based consultant, I must make the most of the opportunities when they present themselves. That may mean temporarily operating in an overload situation, of which I maintain my awareness, but then, gradually, unnoticed, that overload situation becomes the norm, and stress has taken over. A good night's sleep is always helpful, but when we get into permanent overload, the constant state of overdrive, even many good nights of sleep are unavailable to us as we wake up during the night pondering tomorrow's events, rehash today's events, and fret instead of plan.

Insidiously, unnecessary activities are deleted from the busy calendar until only work-related items are there, and only professional purposes are satisfied. Understanding friends know that once the intensely busy period has passed, all will return again to normal, and I'll be back in circulation. Those friends who have not been able to accommodate this pattern have long since parted ways with me. But sometimes eliminating social activities does not release enough time to accommodate the workload, and other activities disappear from the calendar: regularly scheduled medical and dental checkups, workouts, walking—in essence, all the activities that tend to restore balance in my life and keep me physically able to handle the temporary increases in the stress.

I confess that I feel as if I am running merely to keep up and never getting ahead. Rats on wheels seem to make more progress than I do at those times. Yet I continue to work through in the hopes of getting past the overload and into subsequent calm. *Not!* That's when I should be hoarding a few hours each week for a walk in the mountains, exercise at the gym, see friends, and enjoy the diversion and change of pace.

Some consultants have been more successful at achieving balance because of mates who refuse to allow them to become so focused that they lose sight of family and themselves and through discipline as rigorous in their personal lives as in their professional lives. And yet I have continually noticed in other consultants who experience intense project activity an increase in paunch as a project progresses and extracurricular activities are abandoned, so I know it's not just me but an occupational hazard.

I've tried observing other consultants who seem to do better with balance. Mickey Rosenau and his wife, Ellen, have frenetic schedules and cluttered calendars, but each year they schedule trips and time together that is immutable and go off to exotic places for R&R: trekking in Bhutan, scuba diving in the Maldives. Ed and Barbara Stone plan and carry through trips together, away from a demanding business and grueling travel schedule. Jack and Jan Schroeder ski together and go on biking trips—no pagers or cellular phones allowed. Ira Gottfried flies his plane to air shows and ski areas so that he and his wife, Judith, can take advantage of those private, nonwork moments.

I live alone and am now single. While married and raising a son,

I was much more rigorous about vacationing but allowed too much work to interfere with my vacations and private life. *Mea culpa.* I find I still struggle to achieve relaxation time, but my next major hurdle is to make that time. I've tried just taking a break from consulting to recharge my batteries, which helped regain my perspective.

## THE LONELINESS OF THE LONG-DISTANCE CONSULTANT

Especially if you have your office at home, you could go for days without seeing or speaking to another person. If you are anxiously waiting for the telephone to ring with your next prospect, you might develop a sense of abandonment and alienation. You could keep going with this until you've convinced yourself that the phone will never ring again and you've already had your last assignment.

Or you could push away those negative feelings of isolation and bring the outside world in to you by calling people on your Good People list, arranging breakfast with a member of your network, or attending a professional meeting or conference. You could even arrange a quick ski trip with a friend who shares that interest. The choice is entirely up to you. Remember that consulting *is* a lonely profession, but *you* can mitigate the effects of that loneliness by bringing others into your life, if and when you wish to.

## SENSORY DEPRIVATION AND HOW TO LICK IT

There is a dialectic between the solitary time needed to perform an assignment and the sociability required to network and gain the assignment. The successful consultant learns to manage these two different needs to be with people over time and with experience. However, often when involved in performing an assignment, I find myself falling into the syndrome of sensory deprivation: I begin to feel out of touch with other people and the world around me.

I do like my alone time. It renews and invigorates me, hones my skills, and improves my attitude. Especially when I am working on a project, I need to pull in the world and focus tightly on the task at hand. However, sometimes I detect I've had too much of a good thing. I want to hear the laughter of others and see and interact with other people. I'm getting stir crazy from being by myself for *too* long.

The phone won't ring as long as I sit there, nor will that watched pot boil. So when I'm getting just too focused, too edgy, too antsy— my symptoms of sensory deprivation—a quick fix is to talk with someone, but I know that *I* must take the initiative. That's where the benefits of a network come in handy. For example, Jack Schroeder and I have evolved a relationship whereby either of us can call upon the other for the proverbial cup of coffee, which contains that sweetener of understanding of the sensory deprivation attack.

The dangers of ignoring the symptoms are the increased stress of aloneness, of overfocusing on work. Even worse is the depression that comes from being without people for too long—and that's clearly not productive for an effective consultant.

## THE PAUSE THAT REJUVENATES*

We consultants are supposed to be unbiased, independent providers of services. We generally suggest to our clients that our perspectives

*Adapted from Marsha D. Lewin, "The Pause That Rejuvenates," *Journal of Management Consulting*, 6, no. 2 (1988).

and energy levels are finely tuned to their needs. But, look again in that mirror at yourself, and what do *you* see? An overworked provider of services, stressed out and strained from overwork?

Perhaps it's time to sit back and refresh yourself and your ability to provide clear, objective client services. Teachers (and aren't we really teachers?) have long honored the need for a periodic rest for the one-direction service provider. Much more so for consultants who not only are always providing services to clients but are often unable to slow down lest they have lower-than-needed billables, lest there be a much dreaded lull ahead.

By now you're probably saying that such a need doesn't apply to you; you've got it covered. But are you experiencing fatigue? Does your work bore you—another client to help out of the totally avoidable mess? Do you feel stale, as if you've been doing the same old thing or process for so long that it's coming by rote, without the freshness and excitement you once had in your client engagements? And are you impatient with clients, anticipating what they're going to say, then frustrated when they say it?

Just in case one or more of the above symptoms hits home, but you're still denying it's exactly applicable to you, note that the results of ignoring the body and mind when they call for attention from you can be pervasive—and some, irremediable. Personally, you can damage your health and your family relationships. Professionally, if you do nothing, you can wind up obsolete: a technical dinosaur, still holding on to IBM mainframes in a world dominated by superPCs. If you do the wrong thing—more likely when you are not in close touch with your feelings—you can alienate your client base. They are paying you for your assistance, not for obfuscation and intimidation—and certainly not to serve as a test bed for working out your own frustrations.

So often we defer our pleasures until we've "put enough away." That may mean deferring it to our graves. Increased pressure means increased stress on a system that needs renewal. Even the Bible mandated a seventh year of sabbatical for the fields to prevent soil depletion.

We worry, like the farmer, that conditions will not be favorable next year. Such worries often blind us to our own weakening performance on the job. Like a good consulting assignment, the key to a successful sabbatical is planning ahead. Prepare for your sabbatical in the following ways.

## Do Careful Financial Planning

Put aside enough money for a somewhat reduced, but not totally minimalist, lifestyle and business sustenance. For example, allocate enough money to cover secretarial fees, regular mailings, and so forth. Be sure to include enough money for the theater you've never had time to attend, the course in gourmet nouvelle cuisine of the Southwest, and perhaps that Sierra Club trek through the Rockies. I found six months to be appropriate, figuring on a three-month sabbatical, plus another three months to get back in circulation, and for that first fee check to hit our business' books.

## Organize Your Work Life

A sabbatical does not have to mean a vacation, with physical distancing from the office. It can mean an opportunity to organize the office, redo the marketing materials, refocus on competitive threats—all of which may require working eight hours a day in your office—but not after working eight hours of billable client time. And certainly under no circumstances should the sabbatical consist of business as usual. This may be the opportunity to write that book about which you've been dreaming. During my sabbatical, my staff and I continued to accomplish tasks in education, attended various national and local professional meetings, mastered new software and hardware, marketed, and reorganized and updated internal office systems.

## Take Care of Your Personal Life

Lest your family confuse your need for a refresher with mid-life crisis, it behooves you to talk it over with your spouse, children, significant others. They may well experience fears over what it means (Will we ever have roast beef again? Will we be moving to Peoria?), but if you can communicate the temporariness of it and the completeness of the financial planning you've done, you will probably end up with significant support in your own backyard rather than stressful opposition when you need it least.

## Manage Your Expectations of the Process

If you entered the sabbatical as a frog, you're highly unlikely to emerge at the end of the period as a prince—as a slightly tarnished knight, perhaps, but definitely not a prince. You probably will not make radical changes in your lifestyle, but you might be able to take side paths that have always interested you, modifying your schedule so that when you return to the consulting frenzy, you take time for those activities.

## Describe Your Time Off Accurately

I made the mistake of telling someone I was taking the fall season off so that I could figure out what I wanted to do. He understood this to mean I might be selling my business, selling my home, selling my birthright—and was fearful to recommend me too highly to others. An associate wisely said, "Look at this period as an assignment—for yourself. You are tied up and can't accept any other work because you've fully booked yourself." When I realized I was taking a sabbatical, I felt better. Others approved of a sabbatical. While one reviews and reorients during a sabbatical, there's a sense portrayed to others of not losing one's moorings during the meltdown.

## Maintain Your Peer and Friend Networks

Let the word out to your peers and clients that you are taking a sabbatical. It's not a dirty word, and the more they know the length and reason for your absence and unavailability, the more they can be of assistance, both during your respite and when you return refreshed and ready to perform client assignments.

A sabbatical does not mean withdrawing from your customary circles entirely; rather, it may entail being more in circulation because you're under less working stress with clients. You may have to make more conscious efforts to meet with friends if you don't have a common meeting place in the office for a period (especially true when working on-site with clients), but the virtues of a pre-planned breakfast, lunch, or dinner date are many, not the least of which is the opportunity to reacquaint yourself with chatting (without looking for a signature on a contract) and enjoying your food (rather than having to race through the meal to get back to the office).

## Stay Active

Once you've decided to create a sabbatical space for yourself, don't delay. Decide when you are going to start, and when you are going to reenter the consulting orbit.

*Get away* for at least some portion of that period. It's time for fishing, woodworking, gourmet cooking, writing, whatever your special avocation is. And if you don't have one, perhaps a reasonable goal of your sabbatical is to find out what it is—besides work—that "turns you on." While you may never retire (old consultants don't retire, they just give advice), you may find that as you age, having something to do besides frenetic work will prolong your life and improve the quality of it.

Change your contextual roots, physically and logically. By that I mean, allow your mind to soar. Do things you didn't think of do-ing—that hike through the mountains, an overnight at a bed-and-breakfast that you'd gone by dozens of times and never noticed. Maybe even go to, of all things, a rock concert, just to see what's happening. If you've been looking at your management consulting from one perspective, say data processing, why not read a few books or attend a seminar on behavioral aspects of the nineties.

## Calibrate Yourself

Don't give up the *Wall Street Journal* every day if you've enjoyed it for fifty years, especially if it's your link to the ephemeral "real world" out there. Do use your friends to ensure that you are keeping pace with the world events (wouldn't you have hated to miss the exciting news of Eastern Europe's reentry into the world commu-nity?) and with professional items of note. And another type of calibration should be practiced: calibrate yourself against the goals you've set for yourself and this sabbatical periodically. Just to be sure you are moving ahead with your original plan.

## Getting Back in Harness

To everything there is a season, and every exit (but one) has reentry. As it gets closer to restart time be sure that you've gotten your ducks lined up. That first day post-sabbatical may be terrible, but you also just might find yourself looking forward once again to hearing a potential client's voice at the other end of the telephone and seeing a prospect in his office after so long.

Have *reasonable expectations* of what's going to happen at first. You may be one of the fortunate few who will have dozens of clients lined up waiting for your services, but the odds are that you will have to circulate a bit, glad-hand, and talk a bit as you get back into the flow. That doesn't happen overnight and can, in some specialties, take as long as six months. The marketplace's value upon you is not negative because you're not getting a job first thing.

*Balance* your new assignments and the excitement of being back at work again with the perspective you gained during your sabbatical. Just because you're receiving client fees does not preclude your taking an afternoon off to go to the museum. Surprisingly, you can even prolong the positive effects of the sabbatical by including these "bonuses" for yourself.

*Avoid the rat race.* Once you've broken the frenetic habit, try to avoid jumping right back in the pit. If you dislike traffic, avoid scheduling yourself at peak driving hours. While not all clients live in rustic, rural locations, ofttimes you can make it easier on yourself by rescheduling and reorienting your tasks to suit your desires and schedule. You may not be able to avoid the return to the rat race always, but you surely can minimize the amount you spend running the circuit.

A year after I decided to take my sabbatical, I had our most profitable month in many years. My excitement returned about marketing and my assignments. My feelers were definitely more finely tuned, my patience clearly greater. Watching money go out was often scary and sorely tested my belief system and optimism.

Looking back on the sabbatical experience, I feel I definitely needed to do it. I did it. I'm glad I did it—and I suspect I won't wait seven more years before doing it again! While it did work as hoped, the effect was temporary, and slowly the pressure began to build back up.

Although I can't take a sabbatical every year, I can take time off *on a regular and committed basis.* It becomes just another discipline, and probably the most difficult career decision *you* must make—if you are to sustain your career over the long haul. The other component is to ensure that you sustain in your life a few activities that relax you—allow you to "feel good" about yourself—*and are not connected with work.*

## TENDING YOUR GARDEN

Voltaire's Candide liked working in the garden. I've found that doing the laundry has always calmed me. Something about folding those towels and neatly arranging them is renewing. The same is true with making a pot of chicken soup. I know I'm dealing with my stress well when the freezer is overflowing with neat containers of soup. When I was younger, playing in a women's soccer league was a great destressor, though as I have aged, soccer is no longer an option. I tried to substitute tennis for soccer, but even the most understanding of tennis partners could not endure the erratic availability of a consultant. Running has been valuable, although it is not always an option when on-site with clients due to safety issues in some neighborhoods.

Exercise becomes more important as I age, when stretching often must be done consciously. I have a flight of stairs separating me from my office now, and sometimes that may be the only exercise I get all day. There are other ways to build into your schedule a modicum of exercise:

194

- Park away from your destination, to get a bit of extra walking.
- Always use the stairs rather than the escalator.
- Place items on high shelves so that you *must* reach to get them (I'm a small person, so that's quite easy to do).
- When sitting at the computer or desk, get up every hour and stretch your legs and arms.

## YOU ARE WHAT YOU EAT

Lately we have all become much more aware of the importance of diet and exercise in prolonging life and avoiding illness. Low sodium, measured quantities, low fat, less alcohol, no smoking—good-bye to the twenty-four-ounce steak, washed down with dry martinis, by the Marlboro Man. Today's he-man drinks bottled water, has broiled chicken or fish, and works out regularly at the local designer gym.

Today's man (and woman), however, often gets lost in retro-behavior patterns when on assignment: fried chicken, plates licked clean that were overstuffed to begin with, no exercise. And that's the challenge: to sustain these new behaviors, important for our well-being, while involved in the hectic lifestyle that is our norm.

Many gyms have branches in a number of cities or, at a minimum, reciprocal arrangements with other facilities in other cities. Many hotels offer workout rooms for their guests or guest privileges at nearby facilities. Take advantage of them when you make reservations and throw your exercise gear as well as your computer in your suitcase.

Scientific evidence shows that we think better when the endorphins are released during exercise. High blood pressure is reduced by exercise, and dietary regimens have been shown to be effective in reducing many life-threatening diseases. So why wait until you are on the precipice? You can start now, and live longer and with better quality. It's a personal decision that you must implement if you are going to survive. Besides, if you can't justify it on other grounds, you'll do a better job for your clients if you are in good health; you are more productive and can pay better attention.

I've known numerous consultants who did not take care of themselves and paid the price. They were not able to fend off the cumulative stress of this profession. I hope you'll take the necessary steps to prevent you from becoming one of their numbers.

## CONTROL AND OTHER FREAKS

Harry Vonk, a consulting colleague, used to say that control is an illusion. Maybe it is, but it's a comforting one. Since clients respond better to arranged meetings and deadlines that *are* met, a consultant's life eventually becomes a series of deadlines and schedules that can challenge the best barnstorming politician around. At some point a consultant needs to evaluate whether he or she is in control or is being controlled.

We need to allow things to get out of control—to allow for those days when appointments are rescheduled, creating conflicts with other clients; when the car fails us; when the copy store leaves out the middle section of the critical report—and to enable ourselves to greet such events with a sense of humor rather than a display of pique or temper outburst. If we can't get past the inevitable uncontrollables, we'll soon be without clients who hire us for our abilities and professionalism, not our angry outbursts and frustrations.

When things appear to be under control, remember that this is a momentary occurrence that will soon pass. Tomorrow will bring another challenge to your equanimity and sense of order.

# RECOGNIZING STRESS

I've discovered that others can better recognize the stress in me than I can—or at least they can recognize it earlier than I can. Here are some telltale signs for me, and probably for you too:

- My sense of humor disappears.
- I get frustrated easily over trivial things.
- Although exhausted, I can't sleep well.
- Although not hungry, I eat more than usual.
- I feel that I am not being good to myself.
- Although I spend more time working, I don't feel as if I'm making any progress.
- When interrupted, I am impatient.
- I get aches, pains, and colds.
- My anal-retentive qualities are more pronounced than usual.

If you were to ask Max, my office manager and right hand, she'd probably add a few points of her own—none of which are flattering, but each one of which I'd support.

# REDUCING STRESS

When I notice the stress within me, I know I need to stop the world, get off for a bit, and then get back on. My nemesis has been taking time off when I most need it or allowing time for some serendipity to intrude on my life. Of late I've been observing an associate, Keith Kennedy, who manages to sustain an incredible energy and productivity and also attends his daughters' college and high school varsity activities, both local and distant. He has made the time to add other interests to his life, and the benefits show in his productiv-

197

ity and overall well-being. The quality and quantity of his work are inspirational.

When I get too out of balance, I call a halt and set a plan to work my way back toward normalcy: commitment to workout, dinners with friends, read a trashy novel, pick up the old guitar, catch up on the movies I missed, go for a walk along the beach, clean a closet, try a new recipe. The planning is an integral part of my therapy because it allows the light of a calmer future to shine through for me.

A few years ago, in the midst of an important project, I became quite ill and lost my hearing. Fortunately, with good medical care and bed rest for some days, my hearing returned and I recovered completely, but I was a sick—and frightened—consultant. I remember a prospect's calling to find out about our practice and I was totally unable to hear what was being said. Since then I've had occasional early warning symptoms indicating I am run down again; a wiser me takes to the bed *immediately* and rests so that my dreadful experience is not relived.

Learn to recognize the stress symptoms that are your particular alarms, and train yourself to *heed them*. If watching a football game on television is your no-brainer, then zone out on it and renew your batteries. There have been many books and articles published on managing stress, but common sense and awareness of your own process are the best cures of all.

## SPOIL YOURSELF ROTTEN

When we are most in need of it, we seldom do it. We are waiting until the rat race slows down and we can give ourselves a reward for having endured this hectic time. Just to ensure that you do get to that restful nirvana, give yourself some perks along the way: a hot bath (you would have showered anyhow); remove the phone from the hook during dinnertime so that you have some valuable and uninterrupted time with your patient spouse; allow yourself to see that Super Bowl playoff game (even if you have to videotape it and fast forward past the commercials). Spoiling yourself involves ensuring that you pamper yourself when you need a bit of it to keep you going through very difficult times. Figure out what spoils you, and add it to your busy life.

# CHAPTER 11

# Growing Your Business

I just hung up the phone after speaking with a colleague who informed me that after many successful years together, he and his partner were going their own ways. There was sadness, disappointment, reconciliation to the separation, and concern about the future but no acrimony and no arguing over division of profits, ownership of intellectual property, patents, or furnishings and inventory. It was an amiable divorce.

One of the realities of a successful practice is probable growth of that practice: How do you grow it optimally? If you get larger, who will be the manager of others? Because the environment in which we practice is always changing, our practices must change perforce. I've been a partnership, a sole proprietorship, and a corporation. Each one worked best for me at a particular time, and when the organization form no longer best served me because of retirement plans, tax structures, or liability, I changed it. But growth usually means bringing in other people, who want a piece of the business, an equity position, as a sweetener. Otherwise they could run their own business.

Growth is an important and often insurmountable issue for the entrepreneurial consultant. Partners usually mean a loss of independent action, one of the advantages of being an entrepreneur. But they can, under the best circumstances, mean you are able to take on more and larger assignments, reduce the potential of sensory deprivation, and reduce the financial responsibility that rests on your shoulders alone.

The best advice I got on partnerships was from my lawyer brother-in-law, who instructed me to set up the partnership agreement to dissolve automatically after a given period. His argument was that if the partnership was working, we would then have the energy to put into renegotiating the agreement rather than having to put energies into dissolving the partnership. As it turned out, the partnership was not generating the assignments and revenues we'd hoped for, so we automatically dissolved without any hard feelings.

Forming alliances with other firms is a fashionable way of growing today. You look for a company in a related field with which to form a long-term relationship or alliance. Then you make an agreement between you to approach or deal with specified areas, products, or issues jointly for the mutual benefit of both companies. This approach is particularly helpful for companies that need you to complete their offerings. You may fill in that missing function, geography, technology, resource, or qualification that is needed. It's a situation where together you are more than you are individually. If work develops, you're involved.

Alliances work well when you both share ethics, cultural fit, and objectives and have actually worked together. A proposal or mailing done together brings out into the open your individual communication and execution skills. If you are diametrically opposed, it's better to find out early on rather than while trying to perform a client assignment. You could view an alliance as a learning period for each party, with the goal of determining how well you can communicate and therefore how well you can expect to work together in a joint venture or teaming effort in the future.

When deciding to grow, also plan for the inevitable downside so that you do not lock yourself into a financial commitment you cannot support. Seeking legal help at this point is very important. Your personal issues will have much to do with how you solve the growth problem, as you can see from the list of trade-offs in Exhibit 11-1.

You may develop your own list as you deal with growth issues. I prefer the subcontracting relationship for many reasons: within my specialty, new talents are required; obtaining them on a subcontractor basis is better because then I am not responsible for retraining an existing staff, which needs to be upgraded to the constantly new technologies; and since we are project based, the ebb and flow of work makes having a large, full-time staff an unnecessary, but significant, expense.

I've embarked on an informal partnership agreement that is more truly a joint venture. My colleague and I retain our own businesses and share the expenses and profits equally. We have cleft the responsibilities as evenly as possible and attempt to give the client a single view, which is sometimes difficult to do. As we got to know one another's style, there were bumps in the road, but as the trust was established, the bumps evaporated. The project has been successful and enjoyable. Our chief issue to resolve was who was in charge of what, for there can only be one lead horse in the team pulling the wagon if you want to get to your destination. More than once I marveled that two very independent and successful consultants could work as closely as well for so long.

**Exhibit 11-1**
PROS AND CONS OF DIFFERENT GROWTH OPTIONS

| Option | Advantages | Disadvantages |
|---|---|---|
| Use subcontractors | Less administrative and ongoing costs | Not always available<br>Can become competitors |
| Hire employees | Easier to build on known talents | Ongoing cost commitment<br>More administration required |
| Partnership | Shared responsibility: costs, decision making | Shared decision making<br>Shared resources |
| Do it yourself | Autonomy in decision making | Cannot sustain for extended periods of time<br>Stress on yourself<br>Limited resource |
| Form alliance | Expand your marketplace<br>Flexible arrangement<br>Can maintain your own presence as well | Shared decision making<br>Time to determine viability |
| Joint venture | Temporary by agreement<br>Shared responsibility | Shared decision making<br>Shared resources (often) |

# WHAT'S THE RIGHT SIZE WHEN?

You know you're dealing with a size problem when you are simply out of time or you don't have all the talents needed for the assignment. If the talent required is of a small commitment in nature, you can subcontract to another consultant to perform the task. However, if there's an opportunity for an adjunct position on an ongoing basis, you might want to choose from one of the list of options and trade-offs noted in Exhibit 11-1.

If you don't have enough of yourself to go around, then you really need something on a more permanent basis to relieve the pressures on you. Again, you have the list of options to choose from and opportunities for leveraging yourself. If it is project based or situational and temporary, you generally do not want to commit to a long-term relationship and incur long-term responsibility. Since consultants ultimately work on a project basis (although that project can last five to ten years) establishing a large firm may not be the best use of time, energy, and money.

Ira Gottfried established one of the most successful middle-tier consultancies in the West. He grew an information technology specialty from a partnership, to a successful corporation, and then sold it to one of the Big Six. He might not have been able to do so in the climate of the 1990s, but was able to do so earlier. There was significant demand for his type of specialty, which has since been subsumed by many internal capabilities and downsizing within his client base. When I looked toward growing my own corporation in the late 1980s, I saw a shrinking environment and felt the jump from small company to large company was insurmountable. The right size for me was the one I had at the moment.

As a general rule, before you formalize growth legally, establish a trial relationship to see if it's going to survive the test of time. You may find, as did I, that the informal relationship was adequate in and of itself, and no expensive implementations were necessary. A letter of agreement spelling out your obligations to one another, to your clients, and to your subcontractors is always advised, of course.

The secret to successful growth is *controlling* the growth so that it does not deplete necessary resources. If you are spending your time looking at new cities in which to expand and interviewing additional personnel, who will be servicing the clients and looking for new business? Who will be ensuring that the quality and quantity of your current business do not waver? I know many consultants who have tried to start another office in another city, only to shut it within relatively short time periods because they could not sustain the quality in both locations. They were also perceived as interlopers in one location and not committed to their base city. Sometimes the best solution to growth is not to do so.

# MOVING ON*

Sometimes growth requires relocation. Relocation need not become dislocation if you plan for it and execute it as you would any other project. The issue is to get you up and running in your new community without losing touch with your former location. Years later, I continue to get mail addressed to earlier locations.

Recently I moved twice in one year, and each move was quite different. I'd like to call what I did a semirelocation because I moved only fifteen miles away from where my center of the universe had been for over two decades. However, in Los Angeles that's a major move because fifteen miles can take two hours in heavy commuter traffic. The move was more difficult perhaps than I realized because Los Angeles's geographic breadth makes for a more insular group of consultants—out of sight, out of mind. I think that I didn't have the same impetus to delve into new chambers of commerce and networking groups on the other side of the hill because my old

*Excerpted from Mickey D. Rosenau, Jr., Marsha D. Lewin, Richard D. Harvey, and Stanley Press, "Relocating a Solo Practice," *Journal of Management Consulting* 8, no. 2 (Fall 1994): 23–28. Reprinted with permission.

contacts were only a telephone call away. Without the incentive, I didn't do what I probably would have felt I had to do in a totally new community.

I believe that when you're an expatriate, so to speak, people are willing to go out of their way for you and you are willing to make the effort to get over that initial introductory hump. However, that didn't happen because I delayed making those contacts, figuring I'd soon be in the city and would visit my old business and personal associates.

Whether you go to a totally different location or move six streets away, new and professional-looking stationery, proper equipment, and telephone lines forwarded are mandatory. You need to have your client base reach you, and since so many of us are in directories that are many years old, as soon as we move, we present a problem in providing pointers to our new location to the masses we hope follow us.

Although I was moving only a few miles away, I was going into a totally new telephone system in Los Angeles, and the two companies offer totally different products and groupings. An additional problem was that Los Angeles is so big that it has multiple telephone directories. How one lists oneself becomes not only expensive but awkward at best. I spent time scouting around for the closest quick printers. I fortunately did not have to alter my administrative arrangements, since Max, my long-time secretary, actually lived closer to my new location, and moved with me.

Living a mile and a half from the epicenter of the Northridge earthquake became a major factor in having to relocate again one year later. Because of the volume of work and the instability of the area, I decided to move back closer to my old haunts.

While I had planned the first move down to the gnat's eyelash— phones, fax, stationery, and all ready prior to the move-in date— this second move was much more spontaneous. There was little lead time to prepare mailers in advance of the move and have the stationery ready. And without that prior planning, it went as smoothly as the one the previous year with all the planning, probably due to the fact that it was only fifteen miles away. This time, instead of switching over telephones I merely kept the old number on "call forward" to my new number until the new move was completed. I had a post office box in the area, which I kept for the volumes of magazines and journals until I changed to a new box closer to me; I'm in the area periodically and those are not time-critical communications. I picked up my old network again, among those folks who still remain here, and in a safer environment.

All of which proves that under the right circumstances, either method can work!

# CHAPTER 12

# Recap

The purpose of this book has been to acquaint you with what consulting is *really* like and to get you ready rapidly so that you can go out and try your hand and mind at it, hopefully increasing your chances for success. Part One was a quick start, designed to give you just enough to get you going, while Part Two dealt in greater detail with the business issues that make a consulting practice successful in the longer run. Those are the pro-active moves you must make for success. Part Three dealt with those lifelong issues that can affect your desire to continue your consulting career and the quality of the consulting that you perform. They are the more insidious elements that, if not dealt with, will begin to gnaw at you and affect your long-term viability in this profession.

I have been consulting for almost thirty years, nearly all in my own practice. I never did an apprenticeship in one of the Big Six consulting practices as a prelude to opening my own office. I've had to learn what I've put forth on preceding pages through experience—often painful, generally pleasant, but certainly not vicarious. I suspect that you will also learn from your own mistakes, but hopefully they will be reduced by some of the sharing that has been done here. To help you, Exhibit 12-1 is a business checklist summarizing the major items you should attend to.

# WHAT MAKES AN ASSIGNMENT SUCCESSFUL

The factors contributing to a successful assignment are not those that make a successful consultant. Gary Goldstick, a turnaround consulting specialist, identifies three tests of a good assignment:

1. Did you get paid?
2. Did *you* think you really did a good job?
3. Do the professionals with whom you've been working think you did a good job?

What is common, however, is calibrating your personal evaluation with that of the others with whom you come in contact. Despite the manner in which we may conduct our assignments, living solitarily on a mountain top in the Sierras or in a penthouse in Manhattan, we compare ourselves with our peers and don't lose touch with our profession. We are, above all, professionals.

# CHARACTERISTICS OF SUCCESSFUL CONSULTANTS

There is an inexplicable nature to the entrepreneurial consultants who survive their first assignments and decide to make it their life's calling. They are ultimately optimistic, enduring the cyclical nature

**Exhibit 12-1**

BUSINESS PRACTICE CHECKLIST

Legal agreements
    Subcontractor letter of agreement
    Confidentiality agreement
    Letter of agreement/contract
    Noncompete agreement
    Technical nondisclosure agreement
    Partnership or corporation agreements
DBA (fictitious name statement)
Business license
Stationery
    Letterhead
    Business cards
    Compliments cards
Organization functions/role assignments
Records organization
    File names
    Criteria for saving
Financial Records
    Chart of accounts
    Financial statements: Income statement, balance sheet,
        trial balance
    Invoice formats
    Bank account(s) and checks
    Tax ID number
    Resale number
Project management records
    Project profitability
    Status reports

**Exhibit 12-1**

CONTINUED

Sales/marketing

    Company brochure

    Fee schedule

    Letters of recommendation

Press kit

    Capabilities statement

    Project summaries

    Black and white current photo

    Press release

    List of publications, tapes, seminars, talks

    Reprints of articles

Office tools

    Computer/associated peripherals

    Fax machine

    Copier

    Telephone(s)

    Dial-up network access

    Answering machine

Insurance

    Health

    Life

    Disability

    Professional liability

    Office equipment

---

of their marketplace; they are involved with others; they contribute on many different levels to their clients and to their communities. The most successful consultants I know seem to be the most comfortable with themselves: They have an inner core of self-appreciation and sense of who they are that enables them to exude energy that attracts others to them. And who we are determines the types of people we attract.

I have been trying to evolve a profile of the successful consultant and his or her common traits. I've canvassed many successful consultants, who have offered the following list of characteristics:

- Thoughtful.
- Articulate.
- Good communicator.
- Good listener.
- Disciplined.
- Honest.
- Self-starter.
- Motivated by the process of consulting.
- Tenacious.
- Enthusiastic, energetic.
- Self-believer.
- Passionate, excited.

All of these attributes appear to be present in the three characteristics that exemplify a successful consultant:

- Makes money at the profession over time.
- Makes a positive difference for clients.
- Does a good job.

When I asked successful consultants why they feel they are successful in their work, most responses targeted their own sense of professionalism and high standards. Jack Schroeder said that he "doesn't know how *not* to do a good job." He is more demanding of himself than most clients would be. He always gives 150 percent and never stops, always keeping the pressure on himself. He lives out Vince Lombardi's statements that "the quality of a young man's life is measured by his commitment to excellence, regardless of what field he might be in. You don't do things right once in a while. You do things right all the time."

# WHY ARE YOU STILL CONSULTING?

Every so often, it's a good idea to invest some time and effort in self-study. We need to make time in our usually hectic lives to do a periodic assessment of where we are and where we really want to be. I suspect we have all entered consulting for one or more of the following reasons:

- Freedom to set our own schedule.
- Opportunity to develop our own organization.
- Potential to earn more money.
- The prestigious title of management consultant.
- Ability to tell others how to run their businesses better.

But yesterday's advantages may be today's drawbacks. When difficult clients demand continuous, immediate responses, freedom to set schedules generally evaporates in the face of serving our customer base properly. Here are some typical pitfalls:

- Your own organization may entail so much administration and quality control that you do not have sufficient time to practice the specialty you enjoy.
- With the assumption of responsibilities for nonreimbursable functional activities such as marketing, finance, and company management, you generally end up with far fewer billable hours, and you are susceptible to market ebbs. Your counterpart, who is employed, gets paid consistently, while your bank balance rather clearly reflects market conditions.

- Your prestigious title is often diminished by less scrupulous people who claim to be management consultants but clearly have no credentials or ability.
- And how much do you enjoy assignments where the client does not take your advice, albeit paid for and rendered?

However, the outlook need not be grim. Management consultants have access to a diversity of clients, situations, and exciting changes. Whenever I wonder if consulting is still the profession and challenge for me, I remember what Dave Norris told me many years ago when I was doing a periodic self-assessment: "It's exciting. You never know, when you pick up the phone, what's awaiting you!"

The excitement and stimulation of consulting continue to outweigh the occasional disadvantages. It is glorious to awaken to days when I know I may be confused, angry or frustrated but NEVER bored!

Over these many pages I've attempted to give you some practical pointers on how to become a more effective and successful consultant. I've tried to do that by taking as little of your time to get the important points across. As with any client assignment, we can always do more and can always hone our consulting skills. Consulting is a process: Our environment changes, our clients change, the tools we use to deliver our services change. In order to keep up with these changes, we must remain open and continue to work at being the very best consultant we can be. All the rest is merely commentary.

# Associations and Resources for Consulting Accreditation

The *Council of Consulting Organizations*, comprising ACME (Association of Management Consulting Firms, the large firm members), and the *Institute of Management Consultants* (individual certification) are the largest national organizations. The institute certifies management consultants who have practiced for a minimum number of years and satisfied experiential and/or academic requirements, with required references from previous clients. Contact the IMC Executive Director, Claire Rosenzweig, CAE, 521 Fifth Avenue, 35th Floor, New York, NY 10175, 800-221-2557.

The *National Bureau of Professional Management Consultants* is strong regionally (southern California) and has embarked on national delivery of its programs. It has a certification centered around a common body of knowledge for consultants, which is similar to that of the Institute of Management Consultants, and there are requirements to be satisfied. Contact the NBPMC Executive Director, Vito Tanzi, Management Consulting Center, 3577 Fourth Avenue, San Diego, CA 92103, 800-543-1114.

The *Consultants Roundtable* in Los Angeles offers local educational programs for potential and experienced consultants who wish to fine-tune their skills. Contact David Gering, President, 2380 East Birchfield Street, Simi Valley, CA 93065, 805-526-5599.

The *Consultants' Bookstore* is a resource rich in books and materials for consultants. In addition, it publishes the industry newsletter, *Consultants News*, on a monthly subscription basis. Contact James Kennedy, editor, *Consultants News*, Templeton Highway, Fitzwilliam, NH 03447, 603-585-2200, for a list of periodicals and a sample copy of the newsletter.

# BIBLIOGRAPHY

ACME, Editors. *How to Select and Use Management Consultants.* New York: ACME, 1987.

Asher, Donald. *The Overnight Résumé.* Berkeley, CA: Ten Speed Press, 1991.

Bellman, Geoffrey M. *The Consultant's Calling: Bringing Who You Are to What You Do.* San Francisco: Jossey-Bass, 1990.

Carlson, Richard K. *Personal Selling Strategies.* New York: Wiley, 1993.

Cody, Thomas G. *Management Consulting: A Game Without Chips.* Fitzwilliam, NH: Kennedy Publications, 1986.

Connor, Richard, and Jeff Davidson. *Marketing Your Consulting and Professional Services*, second edition. New York: Wiley, 1990.

## BIBLIOGRAPHY

Connor, Richard, and Jeff Davidson. *Getting New Clients*, second edition. New York: Wiley, 1993.

Greenbaum, Thomas L. *Consultant's Manual: A Complete Guide to Building a Successful Consulting Practice*. New York: Wiley, 1994.

Greiner, Larry E., and Robert O. Metzger. *Consulting to Management*. Englewood Cliffs, NJ: Prentice-Hall, 1983.

Gutmann, H. Peter. *The International Consultant*. New York: Wiley, 1987.

Holtz, Herman. *Speaking for Profit: For Executives, Consultants, Authors, and Trainers*. New York: Wiley, 1987.

Holtz, Herman. *The Consultant's Guide to Winning Clients*. New York: Wiley, 1989.

Holtz, Herman. *How to Succeed As an Independent Consultant*, third edition. New York: Wiley, 1993.

Holtz, Herman. *Business Plan Guide for Independent Consultants*. New York: Wiley, 1994.

Holtz, Herman. *The Independent Consultant's Brochure and Letter Handbook*. New York: Wiley, 1995.

Jolles, Robert. *How to Run Seminars and Workshops: Presentations Skills for Consultants, Trainers, and Teachers*. New York: Wiley, 1993.

Karlson, David. *Marketing Your Consulting or Professional Services*. Los Altos, CA: Crisp, 1988.

Kelly, Kate. *The Publicity Manual*. Larchmont, NY: Visibility Enterprises, 1988.

Kelly, Kate. *How to Set Your Fees and Get Them.* Larchmont, NY: Visibility Enterprises, 1989.

Kennedy, James H., editor. *Sample House Organs/Newsletters.* Fitzwilliam, NH: Kennedy Publications, n.d.

Kennedy, James H., editor. *Public Relations for Management Consultants: A Practical Compendium.* Fitzwilliam, NH: Kennedy Publications, 1980.

Kennedy, James H., editor. *The Future of Management Consulting.* Fitzwilliam, NH: Kennedy Publications, 1985.

Kennedy, James H., editor. *How Much Is a Consulting Firm Worth?* Fitzwilliam, NH: Kennedy Publications, 1987.

Kennedy, James H., editor. *Use of Subcontractors in Management Consulting.* Fitzwilliam, NH: Kennedy Publications, 1987.

Kennedy, James H., editor. *The Management Consulting Idea Book.* Fitzwilliam, NH: Kennedy Publications, 1988.

Kennedy, James H., editor. *Fee and Expense Policies/Statements of 46 Management Consulting Firms,* revised edition. Fitzwilliam, NH: Kennedy Publications, 1992.

Kennedy, James H., and David A. Lord, editors. *Management Consulting 1990: The State of the Profession.* Fitzwilliam, NH: Kennedy Publications, 1990.

Kotler, Philip, and Paul N. Bloom. *Marketing Professional Services.* Englewood Cliffs, NJ: Prentice-Hall, 1984.

Lambert, Clark. *The Business Presentations Workbook.* Englewood Cliffs, NJ: Prentice-Hall, 1988.

Marcus, Bruce W. *Competing for Clients in the 90s.* Chicago: Probus, 1992.

Metzger, Robert O. *Profitable Consulting: Guiding America's Managers into the Next Century.* Reading, MA: Addison-Wesley, 1989.

Millar, Victor. *On the Management of Professional Service Firms.* Fitzwilliam, NH: Kennedy Publications, 1991.

Reimus, Byron. *How Management Consulting Firms Are Using Advertising Today.* Fitzwilliam, NH: Kennedy Publications, 1994.

Ruhl, Janet. *The Computer Consultant's Guide: Real-Life Strategies for Building a Successful Consulting Career.* New York: Wiley, 1994.

Schaeffer, Garry, and Tony Alessandra. *Publish and Flourish! A Consultant's Guide: How to Boost Visibility and Earnings Through a Publishing Strategy.* New York: Wiley, 1992.

Schrello, Don M. *The Complete Marketing Handbook for Consultants.* San Diego: University Associates, 1990.

Shenson, Howard L. *The Contract and Fee-Setting Guide for Consultants and Professionals.* New York: Wiley, 1990.

Shenson, Howard L. *How to Develop and Promote Successful Seminars and Workshops: A Definitive Guide to Creating and Marketing Seminars, Workshops, Classes and Conferences.* New York: Wiley, 1990.

Shenson, Howard L. *138 Quick Ideas to Get More Clients.* New York: Wiley, 1993.

Shenson, Howard L. *Shenson On Consulting.* New York: Wiley, 1994.

Smith, Brian R. *The Country Consultant.* Fitzwilliam, NH: Kennedy Publications, 1982.

Tepper, Ronald. *Become a Top Consultant: How the Experts Do It.* New York: Wiley, 1987.

Tepper, Ronald. *How to Write Winning Proposals for Your Company or Clients.* New York: Wiley, 1990.

Tepper, Ronald. *The Consultant's Proposal, Fee, and Contract Problem-Solver.* New York: Wiley, 1993.

Veitch, Thomas H. *The Consultant's Guide to Litigation Services: How to Be an Expert Witness.* New York: Wiley, 1992.

Weitzel, James B. *Personality Traits in Professional Services Marketing.* Westport, CT: Greenwood Press–Quorum Books, 1994.

White, Somers, et al. *Stand Up Speak Out and Win!* Phoenix: The De Green Corporation, 1980.

# INDEX